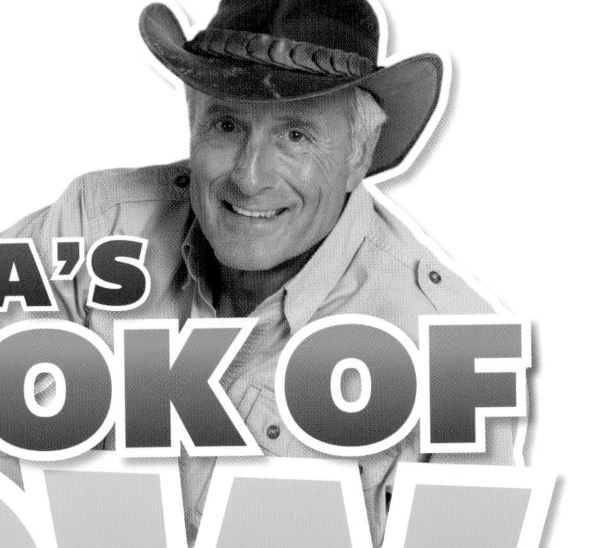

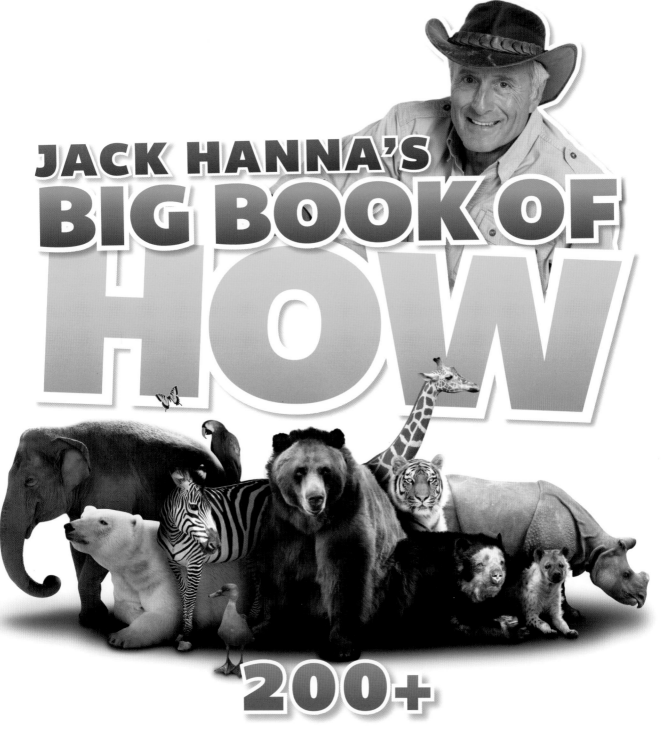

JACK HANNA'S BIG BOOK OF HOW

200+

WEIRD, WACKY AND WONDERFULLY WILD ANSWERS TO YOUR AWESOME ANIMAL QUESTIONS

TABLE OF CONTENTS

Want to learn more? Check out jackhanna.com today!

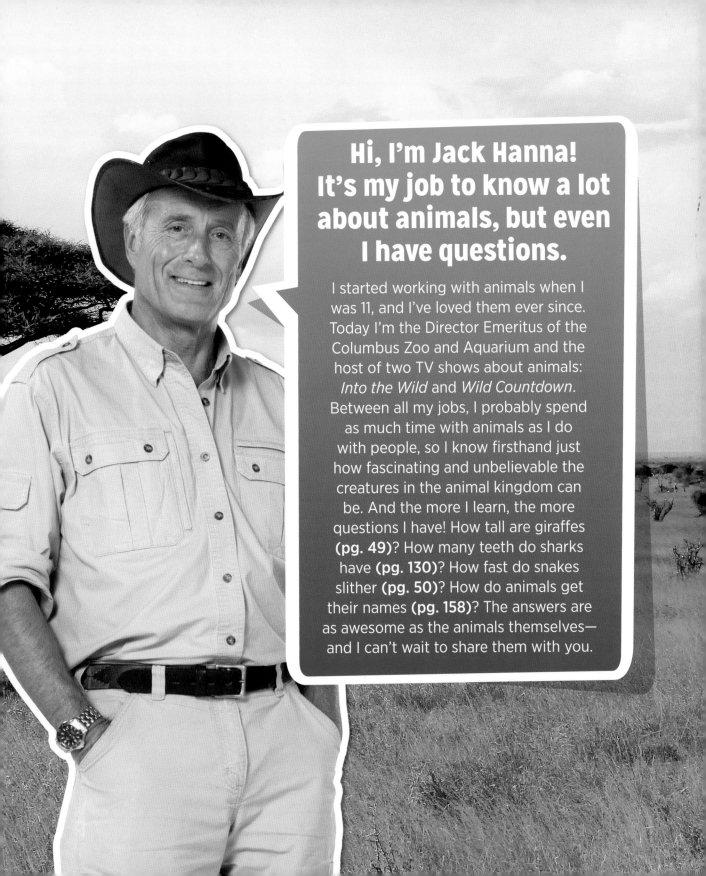

Hi, I'm Jack Hanna! It's my job to know a lot about animals, but even I have questions.

I started working with animals when I was 11, and I've loved them ever since. Today I'm the Director Emeritus of the Columbus Zoo and Aquarium and the host of two TV shows about animals: *Into the Wild* and *Wild Countdown*. Between all my jobs, I probably spend as much time with animals as I do with people, so I know firsthand just how fascinating and unbelievable the creatures in the animal kingdom can be. And the more I learn, the more questions I have! How tall are giraffes **(pg. 49)**? How many teeth do sharks have **(pg. 130)**? How fast do snakes slither **(pg. 50)**? How do animals get their names **(pg. 158)**? The answers are as awesome as the animals themselves—and I can't wait to share them with you.

The Desert

The Grasslands

The Forest

The Rainforest

The Ocean

The Poles

How about these habitats!

A "habitat" is an environment where certain animals live. There are different types of habitats all over the world. Each one provides animals with food, water and shelter. From deserts to oceans, each habitat is unique. They experience different weather, foster the growth of different plants and develop different landscapes. That's why each one is home to different animals! To put it in terms you're familiar with, habitats are like neighborhoods, and each animal prefers one neighborhood over others. Most of the time, the preference has to do with what each neighborhood has to offer. Polar bears have a thick layer of fur and are experts at catching seals and fish to eat, which is why they thrive in the cold and icy weather of the North Pole rather than the hot rainforests in South America. What type of habitat do you want to live in?

Howdy from THE DESERT

DRY DOESN'T BOTHER THESE AWESOME ANIMALS!

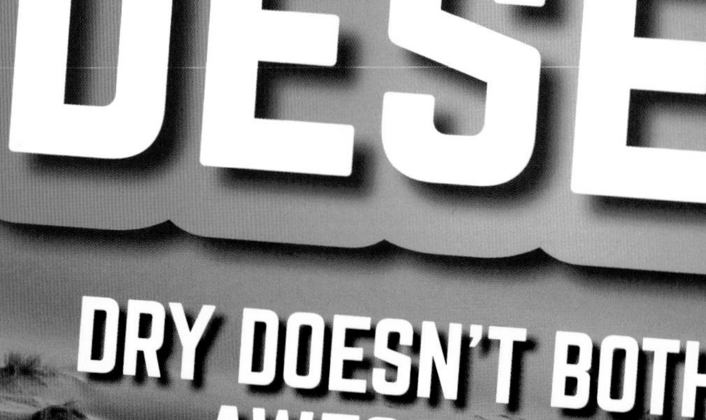

Every continent on Earth features at least one desert region. In some parts of the world, there are whole countries that are comprised completely of desert!

Desert, not dessert!

With less than 10 inches of precipitation each year, deserts are always dry and usually hot. But deserts can be cold sometimes, too. In fact, Antarctica is the world's largest and coldest desert! The largest hot desert, the Sahara, is located in northern Africa. Measuring about 3.6 million square miles, it is almost as big as the United States. There are deserts on every other continent, too. In total, they cover about one third of Earth's land. Deserts are home to unique wildlife that can take the heat—literally! From camels to tortoises to scorpions, every desert animal has mastered surviving the barren terrain's harsh conditions. Here's how!

FUN FACT!
Desert plants go without water for years at a time! But they have long roots underground, so they can get water when they need it.

How do bats fly?

It's difficult to see through darkness, so instead of depending on their eyesight, bats use their mouths to find their way through the night. The trick is called echolocation, and most bats use it to bounce sound off nearby objects and identify their locations—along with the locations of their prey.

Look ma! No night vision goggles!

SOUND IT OUT!

Nocturnal

(NOCK-ter-NAL)

Bats are nocturnal, which means when everyone else is saying "goodnight," their day is just getting started.

FUN FACT!
In a bat's wing, you can find all of the same joints that are in your hand—plus a few more! Bats use these joints to change the shape of their wings as they fly for better control.

How fast are white-tailed jackrabbits?

Many people know jackrabbits for their big ears, but they're also known to be very quick runners. Thanks to their thin bodies and long back legs, white-tailed jackrabbits can run up to 40 miles per hour. When they jump, these energetic mammals can reach heights greater than 11 feet.

WHITE-TAILED JACKRABBIT

DROMEDARY CAMEL

How far can camels travel in a day?

While they may not look like they're moving as fast as other desert animals, camels can travel amazing distances on a daily basis. The average dromedary camel is able to travel up to 100 miles in a single day.

How do vultures find their food?

Even with a good pair of eyes, it seems it would be difficult for birds like vultures to locate prey from way up in the sky. But unlike other birds, vultures don't actually rely on their eyes to spot their meals. Instead, they use their strong sense of smell to find something they can swoop down to pick apart.

WHITE-BACKED VULTURE

How many kinds of camels exist?

Today, there are two species of camels roaming the desert, dromedary and bactrian. You can easily figure out which species is which based on the number of humps on their back. A dromedary camel has one hump, which is almost D-shaped. The bactrian camel has double the humps, and those two humps together make a sideways "B" shape.

DROMEDARY CAMEL

BACTRIAN CAMEL

FUN FACT!
A camel growl was one of the sounds used to make Chewbacca's voice in *Star Wars.*

The humps on a camel's back contain:

A Baby camels

B Stored fat for nutrients

C Saliva

Check your answers on page 172!

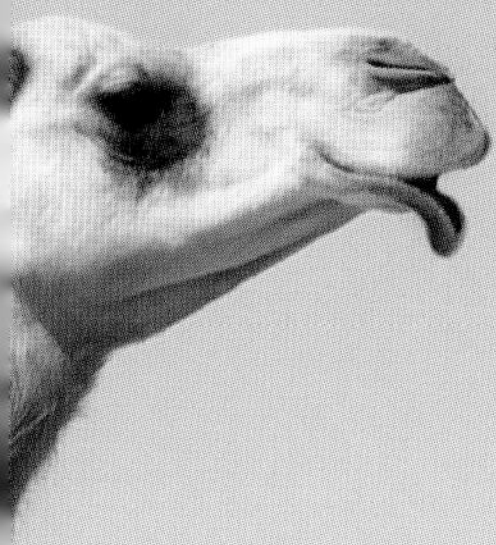

DID YOU KNOW?
When baby camels are born, they don't have humps! But even though it takes a little while for their humps to grow, it takes no time at all for them to be on the move. Just hours after being born, baby camels are able to run.

How slow are tortoises?

Tortoises are super slow. Some travel at only ½ a mile per hour! At that pace, it would take them more than two days to finish a marathon.

LEOPARD TORTOISE

FUN FACT! Terrapins are related to turtles and tortoises, but they spend some time on water and some time on land.

RED EARED TERRAPIN

How are tortoise shells so tough?

Most of the shell is made up of bone! That layer of bone is then covered with plates of keratin, makes up the outermost part of a tortoise's shell. Keratin is the ame material in your fingernails and air! This protein also makes up some ther animals' most noticeable physical haracteristics, including rhinos' horns nd horses' hooves.

ALDABRA GIANT TORTOISE

How do turtles and tortoises use their shells?

The same way you use a bike helmet: for protection! Because they're slow movers, turtles would be easy targets for badgers and coyotes without their suits of armor. Believe it or not, their shells are part of what makes them so slow. Most of their nutrients go toward developing their shells, so there isn't much left to give them the gift of speed.

GALÁPAGOS TORTOISE

How long can tortoises live?

Some land tortoises can live up to 150 years—or longer!

How do desert animals survive the climate?

It's important to remember that animals live in the desert for a reason, not by accident. Their bodies are made for dry conditions. Just look at fennec foxes! They can go for long periods of time without drinking. Instead, they get water from the lizards and insects they eat.

I'm thirsty for bugs!

Where can fennec foxes be found?

A. Sahara Desert

B. North Africa

C. Both A and B

Check your answers on page 172!

How many legs do spiders have?

From tarantulas to black widows, every single spider has the same number of legs: eight.

CHILEAN ROSE HAIR TARANTULA

How are crickets and grasshoppers different?

It's all about antennae: Those skinny feelers at the top of their heads. Crickets have long antennae, while grasshoppers' antennae are short. The way the insects sing is different, too. Crickets rub their wings together to make noise, while grasshoppers use the friction of their hind legs.

FUN FACT!
Although tarantulas might look scary, their bites are actually less venomous than some bees' stings!

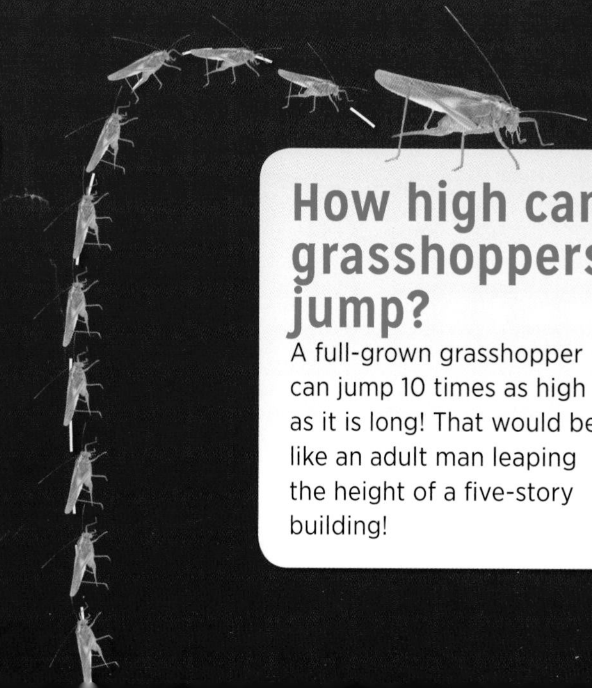

How high can grasshoppers jump?

A full-grown grasshopper can jump 10 times as high as it is long! That would be like an adult man leaping the height of a five-story building!

How do herbivores find food in the desert?

Because very little vegetation can be found in a desert climate, it can be tough for animals who only eat plants to find dinner! Some herbivores, though, like the rabbit-looking rodent known as the viscacha, make the most of their meal opportunities by eating the plants others avoid. One plant they munch on is saltbush, which is way too salty for any other animal to want. Viscachas get rid of most of the salt by removing it from the leaves with their teeth before eating.

VISCACHA

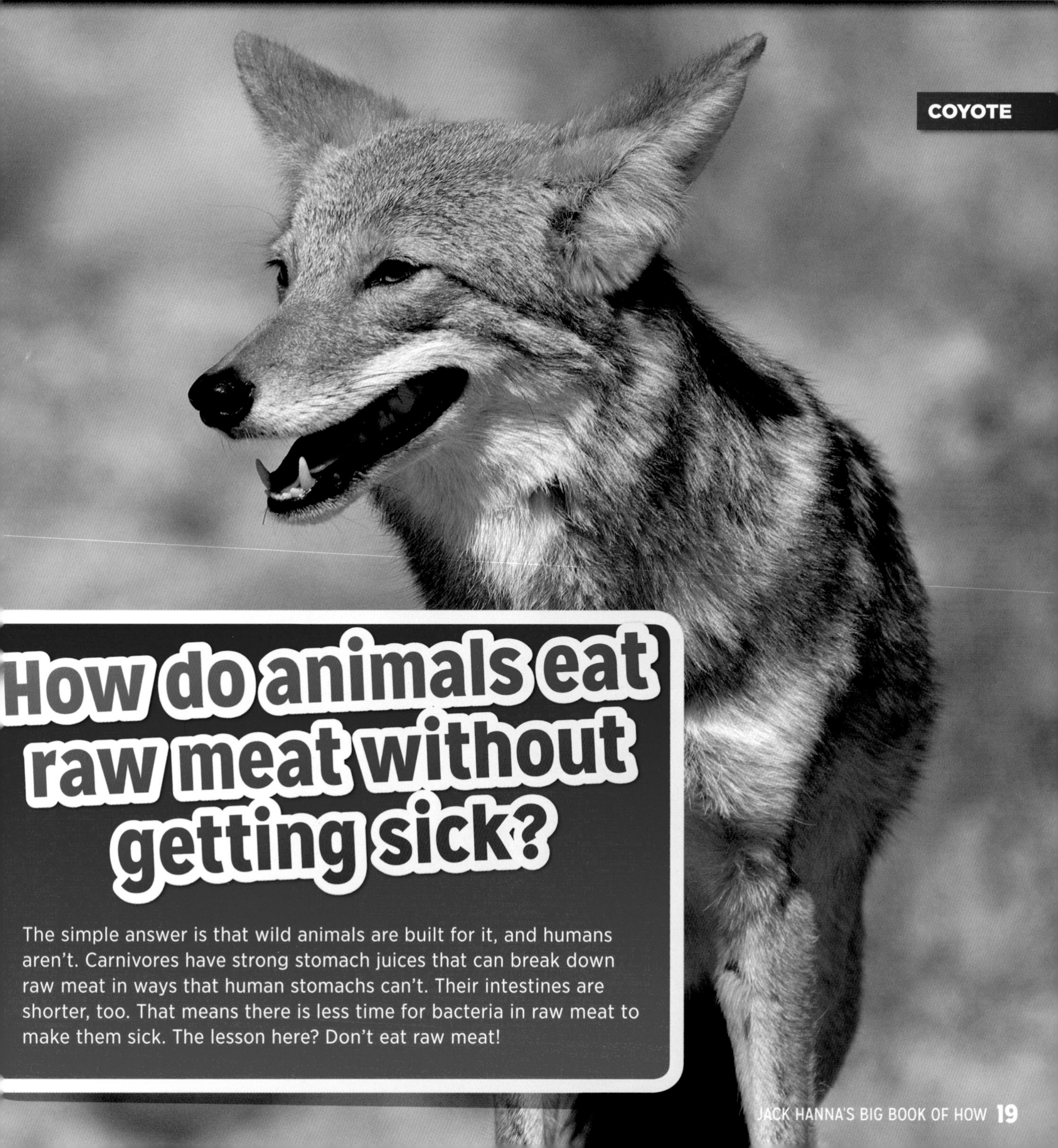

How do animals eat raw meat without getting sick?

The simple answer is that wild animals are built for it, and humans aren't. Carnivores have strong stomach juices that can break down raw meat in ways that human stomachs can't. Their intestines are shorter, too. That means there is less time for bacteria in raw meat to make them sick. The lesson here? Don't eat raw meat!

PUZZLE

This is the word we use for a bat's pointy teeth:

G F A N S

Check your answers on page 172!

How many different bat species are there?

While scientists are still figuring out the exact number of bat species that exist, they do know there are more than 900. Some believe there may even be as many as 1,200 different types of bats flying around the world. Bats are usually divided into two categories based on their size: megabats and microbats. Megabats are larger while microbats refer to the smaller varieties.

FUN FACT!
Bats are the only mammals that can spread their wings and fly.

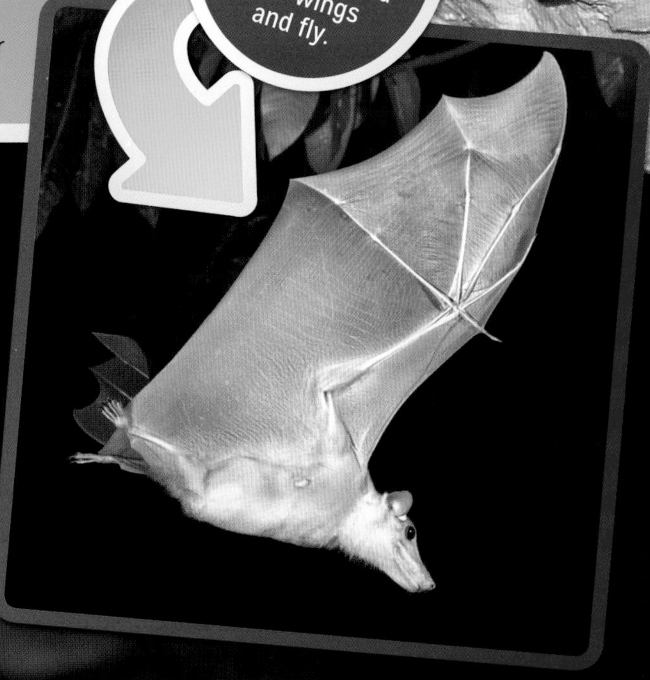

We'll make them
an offer they
can't refuse.

How many meerkats live together at a time?

Meerkat communities can number up to 40. A group of meerkats is called a mob or a gang because there are so many of them!

DID YOU KNOW?
Even though they live in extremely hot climates, meerkats are able to keep cool in the burrows they build. These burrows are made up of tunnels and rooms that the meerkats travel between to stay out of the sun. Each year, the burrows are even used to welcome new meerkats to the family as the females give birth to two to four babies at a time.

How many legs do scorpions have?

Scorpions, like spiders, have eight legs along their bodies. Unlike humans, these dangerous little desert dwellers don't have any bones in their legs—or anywhere else in their bodies. They have an exoskeleton made of chitin instead, which is similar to the shell of a shrimp.

How often do snakes shed their skin?

Snakes spend a lot of time underground, but when they do come up to the surface, it's usually to shed a layer of skin. They do this anywhere from every three weeks to every two months, depending on how fast they grow. Another reason for shedding their skin is to heal any injuries they might be dealing with.

BUSH VIPER

How do zookeepers stay safe when working with animals?

Zookeepers work with many different types of animals every day, and safety is a top priority! They always come prepared to work for the day wearing the proper uniform, carrying the right tools and taking the correct precautions. Each animal is different and has different needs—zookeepers are experts at knowing how to feed, clean habitats and enrich the animals to increase natural behaviors! Two of my grandkids, Gabriella and Jack (left), learned all about animal care and safety at the Wildlife World Zoo when we filmed for *Jack Hanna's Into the Wild* in 2014!

How do owls line their burrows?

Burrowing owls get their name for the tunnels they make and live in, which are called burrows. But because they live in deserts, which are pretty limited environments, you might be wondering where they get materials to make these homes. After they dig their tunnels, these owls line the entrances with mammal dung. This not only keeps the climate inside the nesting place cool, it also attracts insects for them to eat.

BURROWING OWL

FUN FACT!
Gila monsters are venomous! But they don't usually use their venom to kill their prey. Instead, they typically use it as a defense against predators who are trying to eat them.

DID YOU KNOW?
The gila monster is the largest lizard native to the United States! They can grow to be 2 feet long!

Which desert animal does not live underground?

- **A** Meerkat
- **B** Burrowing owl
- **C** Vulture

Check your answers on page 172!

How do snakes control their fangs?

Let's use rattlesnakes as an example. When they're not about to attack, rattlesnake's fangs bend up and lie flat on the roof of their mouths—kind of like a folding chair.

WESTERN DIAMONDBACK RATTLESNAKE

BLACK-NECKED SPITTING COBRA

How do snakes inject venom?

Not all snakes are venomous, but those that are use their teeth to inject venom. One common venomous desert snake is the rattlesnake. When its fangs bite down, muscles in the rattlesnake's face squeeze venom through the fangs from sacs at the roof of its mouth. Some snakes, like the black-neck spitting cobra, can even spit venom at predators. These cobras have special fangs with holes, and when they're threatened they can squeeze out venom at a high pressure, causing it to fly out of their mouths!

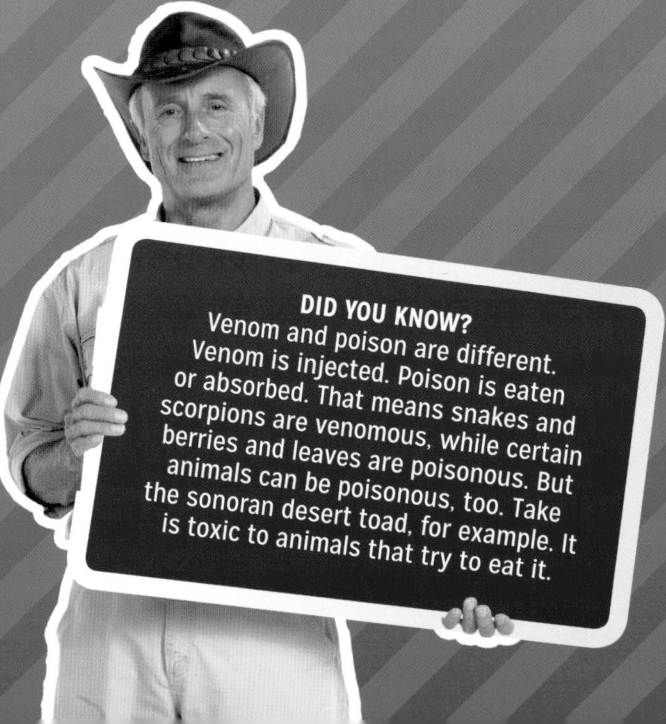

DID YOU KNOW?
Venom and poison are different. Venom is injected. Poison is eaten or absorbed. That means snakes and scorpions are venomous, while certain berries and leaves are poisonous. But animals can be poisonous, too. Take the sonoran desert toad, for example. It is toxic to animals that try to eat it.

Come visit THE GRASSLA

THE CRITTERS WHO LIVE HERE ARE INBETWEENERS!

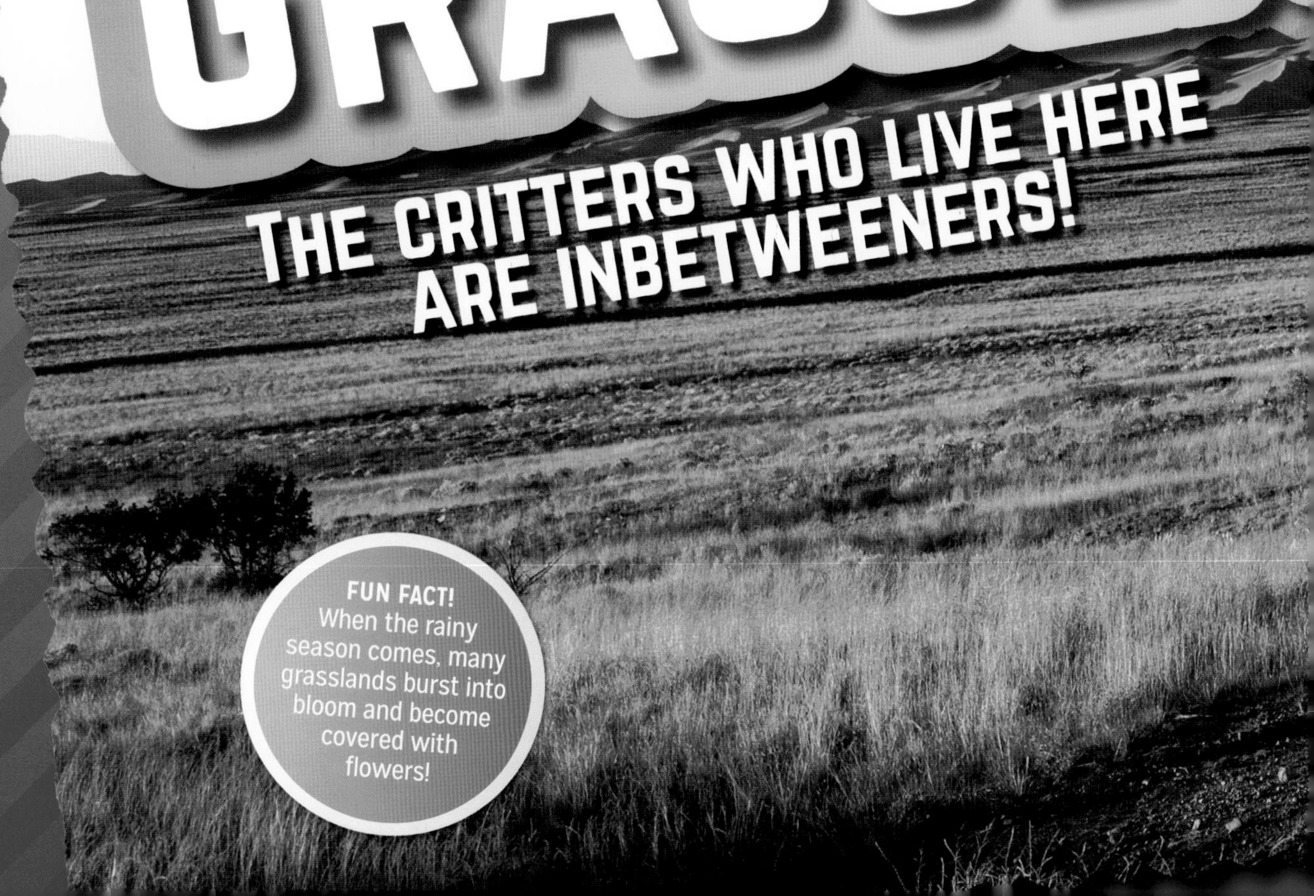

FUN FACT!
When the rainy season comes, many grasslands burst into bloom and become covered with flowers!

NDS

That's a lot to mow!

Grasslands, prairies, rangelands, pampas, savannahs—they're all the same. No matter what you call them, every grassland shares certain characteristics. They get too little rain to be a forest and too much rain to be a desert. So it makes sense that most grasslands are sandwiched between those habitats. Although different grasslands are filled with similar plants, each is home to different animals. That means you won't find cows and horses living in the same space as lions and elephants. Cows and horses live on prairies, while lions and elephants call savannahs home.

How long can cheetahs run at top speed?

Cheetahs can run at top speed for about 30 seconds at a time. However, it's a myth that cheetahs can't run at top speed for long distances because they overheat! Scientists don't know exactly why cheetahs stop after roughly 30 seconds, but the common explanation of a poor internal cooling system has been proven wrong.

27.8
mph

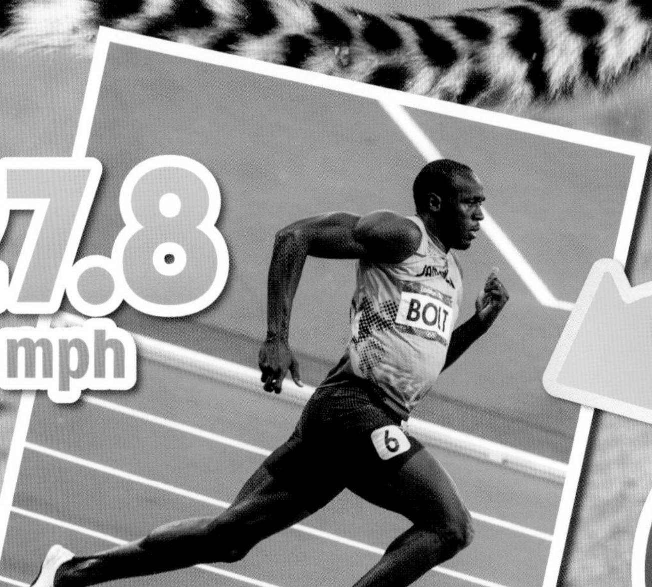

FUN FACT!
Cheetahs are the fastest land animals on the planet. They can run up to 70 miles per hour—more than 2 times quicker than the fastest human, Usain Bolt, who once ran 27.8 mph!

The cheetah Kvamme races around the Heart of Africa watering hole at the Columbus Zoo and Aquarium!

AFRICAN ELEPHANT

How do elephants use their trunks?

Elephants use their trunks for almost all their needs! Most obvious uses include smelling, sucking up water to spray into their mouths, feeding themselves and lifting things. But did you know baby elephants will suck on their trunks for comfort, like a human baby would use a pacifier or his or her thumb? And adult elephants will wrap their trunks together upon meeting—just like a handshake!

DID YOU KNOW?
You shouldn't believe everything you see on TV! For example, these huge herbivores don't actually eat peanuts.

Elephants have better noses than bloodhounds! Can you guess from what distance they can smell a water source?

- **A** 7 miles
- **B** 12 miles
- **C** 18 miles

Check your answers on page 172!

How do prairie dogs survive the winter?

Prairie dogs live in underground burrows with their families. This protects them from both predators and cold, snowy winters! The white-tailed prairie dog will hibernate for up to six months, living off the fat stores they built up during the warmer weather.

WHITE-TAILED PRAIRIE DOG

RED KANGAROO

How do kangaroos protect themselves?

Except for humans and wild Australian dogs called dingoes, kangaroos don't have many natural predators. But when they are threatened, they pound their strong feet on the ground in warning. If you hear that, run! Otherwise, you might get a kangaroo kick or bite.

How did the rhinoceros get its name?

Rhinos are easily pointed out by their horned snouts, so scientists combined the Greek word "rhino," meaning nose, with the Greek word "ceros," meaning horn, and voilà! We have rhinoceroses.

WHITE RHINOCEROS

How many lions live in a pride?

As few as three or as many as 40 big cats make a pride. Prides are made mostly of lionesses who are usually related and their cubs, with only a few adult males per group. Prides are smaller in drier climates than in ones that have more food and water.

We're just lion around!

FUN FACT!
Lions are the only cats that live in large social groups. Other cats prefer to be alone.

The Columbus Zoo and Aquarium welcomed six cubs in 2015!

How much do lions eat?

Male lions eat most, so they get first dibs. They need about 15 pounds of food per day. Lionesses, who eat next, need a little more than 11 pounds. Cubs eat last, and they take whatever leftovers they can get! Hopefully that's not how it goes at your house.

FUN FACT!
Tigers, lions' closest relatives, are just as loud as lions. You can hear both big cats' roars more than five miles away!

How loud can lions roar?

Lion roars can reach up to 114 decibels. That's even louder than a car horn!

114 decibels

PUZZLE

Instead of roaring, house cats do this.

E O W M

Check your answers on page 172!

DID YOU KNOW?
Only some cats can roar: lions, tigers, jaguars and leopards. That's because those species have a special tissue in their throats that other cats don't.

AFRICAN ELEPHANT

How do elephants remember things so well?

It's a mystery why elephants can remember things so much better than other animals. But, boy, can they! Elephants can recognize as many as 30 friends at a time, and their memories last for decades. Researchers think elephants' memories are a big part of how they survive in the wild.

FUN FACT! A group of elephants is called a herd.

Our Columbus Zoo male Asian elephant named Hank is bigger than most—he is more than 15,000 pounds!

How big are rhinos?

Rhinos can weigh up to 6,000 pounds and usually stand about 6 feet tall. An elephant can eat a rhino's weight in plants every 10 days.

WHITE RHINOCEROS

How big are elephants?

Usually weighing between 5,000 and 14,000 pounds and standing up to 13 feet tall, African elephants are the largest land animals on earth. They are a little bit bigger than their cousins, Asian elephants, who can weigh 11,000 pounds and stand up to 13 feet tall.

AFRICAN ELEPHANTS

How large are baby elephants?

They're big, too. Baby elephants can weigh more than 200 pounds and stand 3 feet tall!

How high can kangaroos jump?

Red kangaroos can leap at least 6 feet high in one jump. They're talented long jumpers, too. One bound can shoot them 25 feet forward—or farther!

Can you guess which sentence is true?

A. Kangaroos are an official Australian emblem

B. Kangaroos are left handed

C. Both A and B

Check your answers on page 172!

RED KANGAROO
FUN FACT!
Fleas have even more hops than kangaroos. They can jump up to 200 times their height. That's like a 6-foot-tall man jumping to the top of the Empire State Building's top observation deck.

How do zebras use their stripes?

Scientists aren't positive why zebras have such distinct stripes, but they have a few theories! Zebra stripes might be confusing to predators, who have trouble distinguishing one zebra from the herd, or they might have to do with keeping zebras cool in the hot sun. Some scientists also think their stripes help zebras avoid disease-carrying flies—we don't know why, but flies have a hard time recognizing striped surfaces!

What do zebras eat?

A Plants

B Animals

C Plants and animals

Check your answers on page 172!

FUN FACT!
Underneath its hair a zebra's skin is black.

How are zebras different than horses?

Zebras and horses are both equine animals, which makes them cousins. Their biggest difference is obvious: They don't look the same! Zebras are also less common and harder to tame than horses. Comparatively, they can be pretty unpredictable, and saddles don't fit their bodies well.

SOUND IT OUT!

Equine (EH-kwine)

"Equine" means to belong to the Equidae family. That includes horses, donkeys and zebras.

The Grasslands

MASAI GIRAFFE

PUZZLE

Giraffes live on this continent:

F R C I A A

Check your answers on page 172!

FUN FACT!
A giraffe hoof is nearly as big as a dinner plate—12 inches in diameter!

How do giraffes use their necks?

Giraffes' long, lanky necks are important in making sure they get enough to eat. Instead of fighting for low-hanging leaves like most of the animal kingdom, the herbivores use their necks to snag leaves that hang high in treetops. This is especially handy when food is scarce!

ROTHSCHILD GIRAFFE

How do baby giraffes learn to walk?

They're born knowing how! The 6-feet-tall giraffe calves need only about an hour before they can stand up and walk on their own. Before the day's over, they can run with their mothers. This natural ability helps protect them from predators who would take advantage if they were immobile. Talk about fast learners!

ROTHSCHILD GIRAFFES

FUN FACT!
Giraffes can moo, hiss, roar and whistle.

How tall are giraffes?

Giraffes can grow up to 19 feet tall. That makes them the tallest animal on earth! Their legs alone are about 6 feet in length. Even a giraffe's tongue is long—it's about 2 feet!

DID YOU KNOW?
There's no hiding from predators when you're as tall as a giraffe! Instead, they hang out in groups to stay safe. If they have to defend themselves, giraffes use a karate-style kick. But giraffes don't have many predators, with the exception of lions and crocodiles, because they can run up to 35 mph!

How fast do snakes slither?

Different snakes travel at different speeds. Black mambas are one of the fastest snakes in the world. They can slither up to 12.5 miles per hour! They usually use their speed to escape predators, not to chase prey.

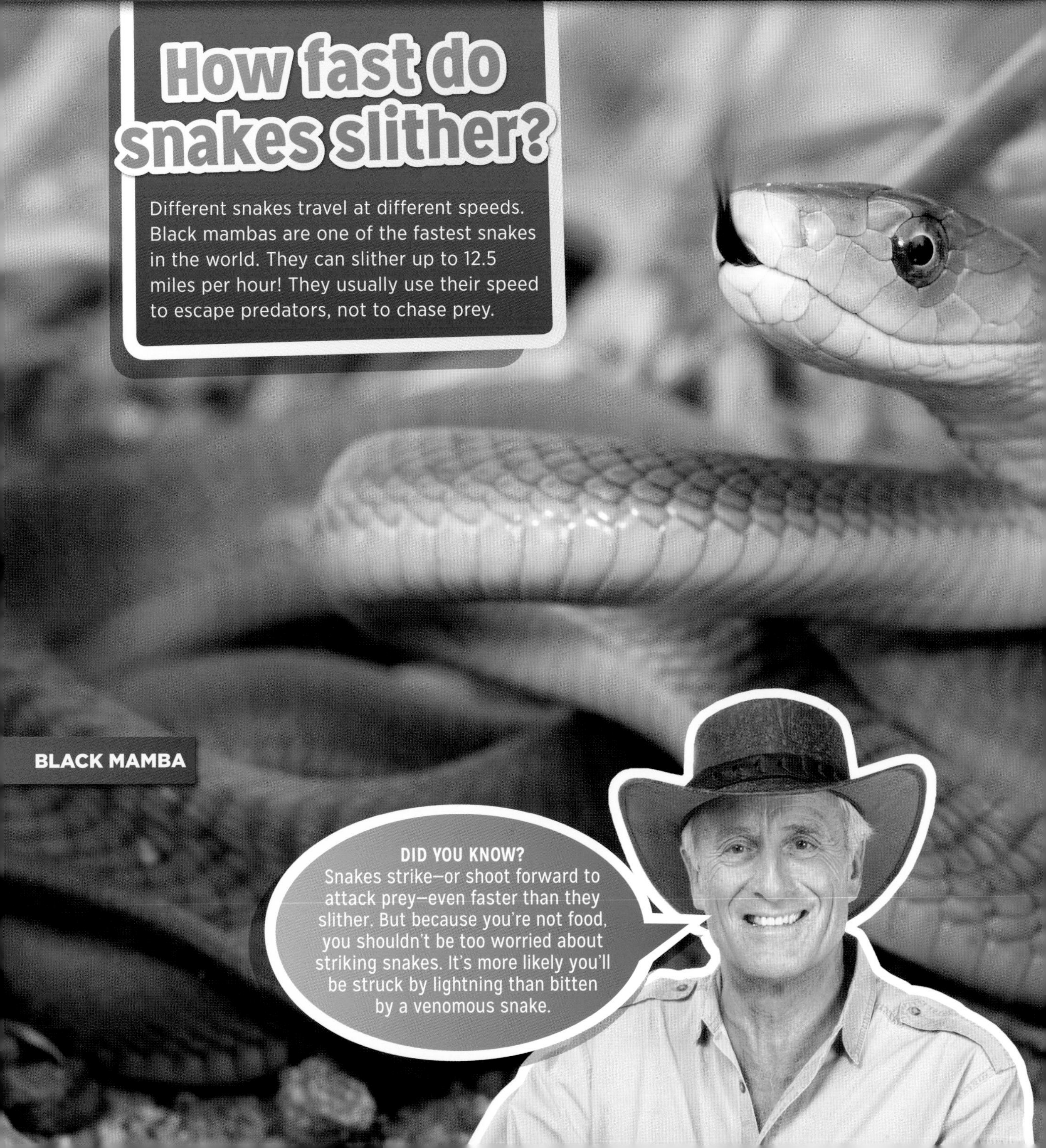

BLACK MAMBA

DID YOU KNOW?
Snakes strike—or shoot forward to attack prey—even faster than they slither. But because you're not food, you shouldn't be too worried about striking snakes. It's more likely you'll be struck by lightning than bitten by a venomous snake.

FUN FACT!
Black mambas were given their name because the inside of their mouths is an inky-black color.

50 mph

How fast are antelopes?

Pronghorn antelopes can reach speeds of more than 50 miles per hour to outrun predators! That makes them the second fastest land mammal, just behind the cheetah. When it comes to long distances, pronghorn antelopes can keep a pace of about 25 miles per hour.

SIBERIAN TIGER

FUN FACT! Tigers are the largest big cats.

How are big cats different than house cats?

Tigers share more than 95 percent of their DNA with house cats! But the small portion of their DNA that is different accounts for a lot of differences. Big cats are larger, faster and more powerful than their domestic counterparts. They're more aggressive, too! Their stomachs are filled with proteins and chemicals that allow them to enjoy different diets than house cats. Finally, big cats roar and house cats meow. Remember, it's all in the genes.

How do cats purr?

House cats and some big cats, like the cheetah, purr by contracting muscles called their larynx and their diaphragm. Scientists aren't yet sure how cats control those muscle movements, but they do know cats purr to communicate.

CHEETAH

How do cats land on their feet?

Cats usually—but not always—land on their feet. They can do this because they're born with flexible backbones and a great sense of body positioning. In other words, it's natural!

FUN FACT! House cats and tigers shared an ancestor nearly 11 million years ago.

BENGAL TIGER

How many stripes do tigers have?

Tigers can have more than 100 stripes! But those stripes are never laid out the same way. Every tiger has its own unique stripe pattern.

How big are ostriches?

Ostriches can be as big as 9 feet tall and weigh up to 350 pounds! That makes them the biggest birds alive today by far.

FUN FACT!
Ostriches have the largest eyes of any land animal. One of their eyes is about as wide across as two quarters.

How do ostriches use their wings?

Ostriches' huge bodies don't lend themselves to flight. Instead, they use their wings to attract mates and to balance while they run. The big birds can reach up to 40 miles per hour!

DID YOU KNOW?
Ostriches don't have teeth, so they swallow stones in order to grind their food. Adult ostriches can carry roughly 2 pounds of stones in their stomachs!

How are bison and buffalo different?

Actually they're pretty similar. Bison and buffalo are members of the same family: Bovidae. Because they look a lot alike, they're often confused for the same animal. But the two animals live in different places and vary slightly in appearance. Bison can be found in North America, but buffalo are native to Africa and Asia. Another difference is that bison have humps on their backs, and buffalo don't.

BUFFALO

BISON

DID YOU KNOW?
Buffalo and bison are grazers who eat tons of plants. In fact, they eat so much that they have to move from place to place to find grass they haven't mowed—I mean eaten.

How fast is a bison?

Although a bison can weigh as much as 2,000 pounds, they can run as fast as 35 mph! They can also change directions quickly and even jump over fences!

How did buffalo wings get their name?

Don't worry: Those delicious snacks aren't made from buffalos. Really, they're chicken. The food was created in Buffalo, New York, so that's where the name came from.

How do cows make milk?

Like just about every other female mammal, cows naturally produce milk after they give birth. Cow milk production happens in their udders, in four separate compartments! A cow can produce about 8 gallons of milk per day. Udder-ly amazing!

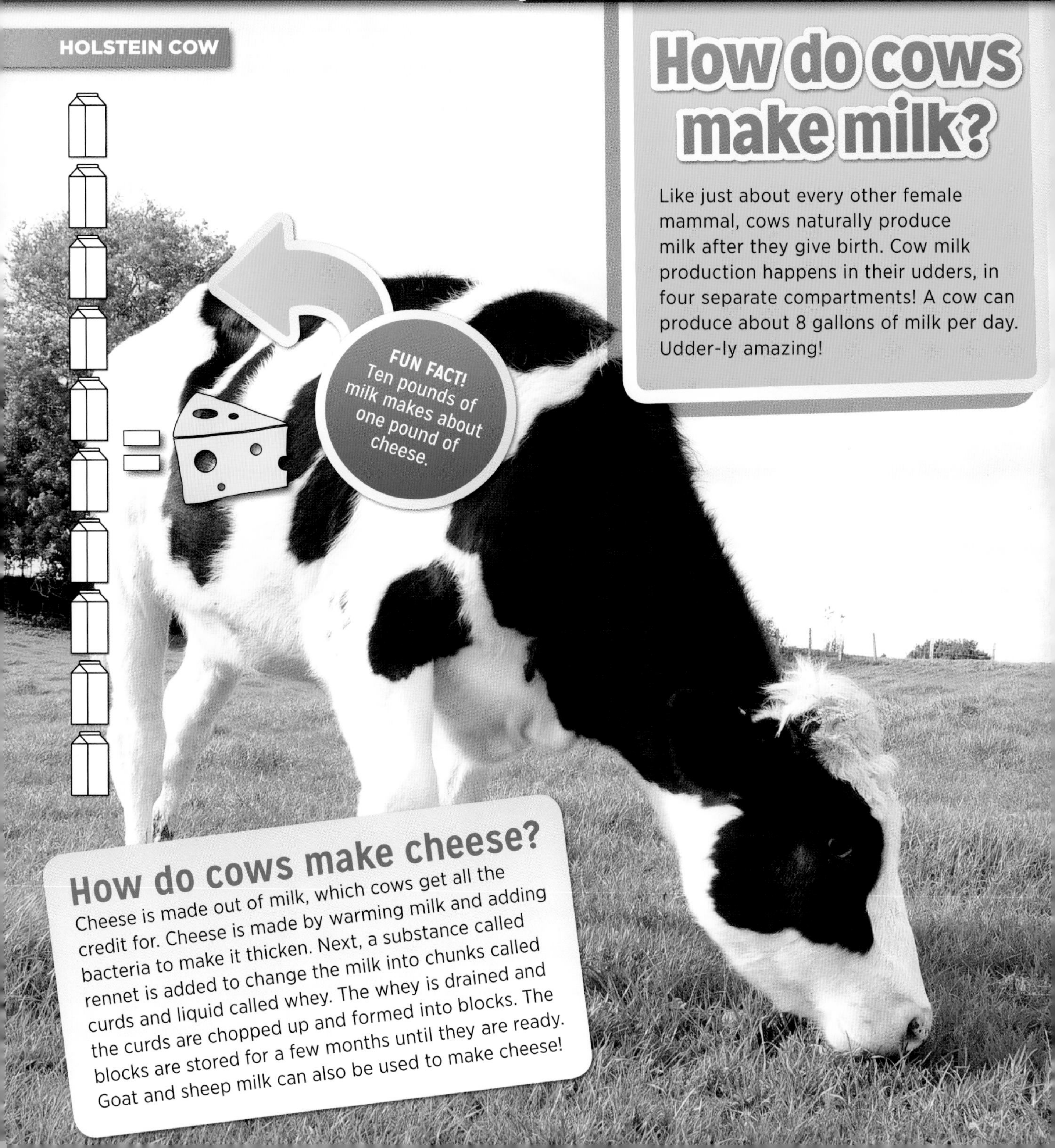

HOLSTEIN COW

FUN FACT! Ten pounds of milk makes about one pound of cheese.

How do cows make cheese?

Cheese is made out of milk, which cows get all the credit for. Cheese is made by warming milk and adding bacteria to make it thicken. Next, a substance called rennet is added to change the milk into chunks called curds and liquid called whey. The whey is drained and the curds are chopped up and formed into blocks. The blocks are stored for a few months until they are ready. Goat and sheep milk can also be used to make cheese!

How long have people ridden horses?

Horses have been domesticated for 10,000 years! These magnificent animals were first kept as pets and used as a way to get around in what's now Europe and Asia. They even appear in cave paintings.

How old can horses get?

Most domestic horses live about 25–30 years. But the oldest horse on record, Old Billy, lived to the ripe old age of 62!

Hello from THE FOREST

THESE CREATURES HANDLE THIS TEMPERATE HABITAT WITH EASE.

FUN FACT!
Many of the trees living in temperate forests are deciduous, which means their leaves change color and fall off in autumn.

The seasons, they are a'changing!

Most temperate, or mild, forests exist in North America, Asia and Europe. The tree-filled habitats receive about 30 to 60 inches of precipitation each year and have four seasons, each with different weather. Unlike other habitats, forests don't see extreme temperatures, which makes life easier for the animals that live there! From the rabbits and bears roaming the forest floor to the squirrels frolicking in the trees to the birds flying above it all, forest animals are as diverse as the habitat itself—and that's how they thrive!

How do owls chew with no teeth?

Owls tear food apart with their beaks or sometimes even swallow it whole, just like a snake! But this is rough on an owl's stomach, so they vomit up pellets of hair and bone, which they can't digest. It might sound gross, but these pellets have helped scientists figure out what owls eat.

FUN FACT! Owls have special feathers that make their flight almost noiseless!

BIG EURASIAN EAGLE OWL

BLACK CAPPED CHICKADEE

How do birds find food?

It depends on the bird. Robins, for example, tilt their heads, listening and also looking around for juicy worms moving beneath the soil. But not all birds consider worms a delicacy. Chickadees will spend a lot of time foraging through trees for plants and berries. Some birds simply catch insects out of mid-air.

How large are beaver dams?

It varies! Beaver dams, which block off rivers and create small personal ponds, can be 6 feet tall and hundreds of feet wide! In addition to building these dams, beavers will also construct a lodge or den for their family. Talk about being busy!

NORTH AMERICAN BEAVER

SOUTHERN FLYING SQUIRREL

How far can flying squirrels fly?

Although flying squirrels don't technically fly, they use their extra skin membrane to glide from tree to tree. These little squirrels can travel through the air for 150 feet. That distance is the length of four school buses!

How do bees make their hives?

Before bees build a hive, they have to find the perfect place for it. Hollow openings in trees work great. The starting places must be big enough to hold about six and a half gallons, with an opening that isn't too large but is big enough for bees to clear out any waste. The opening should face south and sit out of predators' reach. After bees scout the perfect place for their hive, they start making beeswax to create combs by releasing the wax from their stomachs. Starting at the roof and working their way down, they attach combs, which are perfect hexagons, to form the hive.

FUN FACT! A basic bee hive is made of more than two and a half pounds of beeswax!

BUMBLEBEE

How many bees live in a hive?

Depending on its size, researchers think a single hive can house up to 80,000 bees! But that's only in the summer. In the winter, when resources are scarce, the population of a hive can drop below 10,000.

DID YOU KNOW?
There are three different kinds of bees in every hive: the queen, the workers and the drones. Each hive has only one queen. She's in charge of laying all the eggs. Workers are female bees who find food, build the hive and clean the air. They're probably the only bees you'll see outside the hive. Drones are the last kind of bee. They're all male, and they help the queen lay eggs.

How do bees make honey?

HONEYBEE

The process starts with a visit to a flower. Multiple flowers, actually. Bees suck sugary nectar from the flowers with their tongues and store it in something called their honey stomach, which is separate from their normal stomach. When they're full, they head back to the hive and pass the nectar off to bees inside the hive, who take turns chewing it until it becomes honey. Next, they store it in honeycomb cells and fan it with their wings to dry the honey into a sticky paste. Finally, they close the seal with wax to keep the honey, which is their food source, clean.

To make one pound of honey, a hive of bees flies about 55,000 miles. That's about __ trips around the world.

A 1

B 1.5

C 2

Check your answers on page 172!

How much honey do bees make?

A hive can produce about 60 pounds of honey per season, thanks to the huge number of bees that live there. It takes eight bees their entire lifetimes to make one teaspoon of honey.

FUN FACT! You shouldn't feel guilty for eating the bees' dinner. Lucky for us, they make up to three times more honey than they need.

How do bees fly?

In the early 1900s, scientists said bee flight should be impossible! They were puzzled by how the little wings kept the big insects in the air. But researchers now know the secret of their flight lies in the short, choppy flapping of their wings at incredibly fast speeds—about 230 times per second.

230 times per second

The Forest

How do birds fly?

Well, the wings help. A lot. The shape of birds' wings causes the air moving above them to push down with a weaker force than the air moving below them. Birds have tons of other features that help, too. Their lightweight, sleek, inflexible bodies make flying a breeze.

MEXICAN GREY HAWK

How do birds know to migrate?

For birds, migration is an instinct, much like hibernation is for other animals. Migration means to move from one place to another at certain times of the year. Instincts are automatic behaviors that help with survival. When the days start to get shorter, they know to head somewhere warmer because winter is coming.

Hey! I can see my house from here!

FUN FACT!
Birds are the only animals with feathers.

RED-TAILED HAWK

How do hummingbirds fly backward?

Most birds can fly, but only hummingbirds can fly backward! They can do this because they have super light and hollow bones. The way they hold their bodies—upright—and the speed at which they flap their wings—53 beats per second—helps, too. As if that weren't impressive enough, they can fly upside down and hover, too!

FUN FACT!
Hummingbirds get their name for the "hum" sound their wings make when they flap.

ANNA'S HUMMINGBIRD

Can you guess how many different kinds of hummingbirds there are?

- **A** 328
- **B** 832
- **C** 283

Check your answers on page 172!

Sue and I filmed hummingbirds in Ecuador for *Jack Hanna's Into the Wild* in 2015!

How tiny is the world's smallest bird?

The world's smallest bird is the bee hummingbird, and it grows to be only around 2.5 inches—it weighs less than a penny! On the other end of the spectrum, hummingbirds belong to the world's biggest bird family—the Trochilidae family. Now, that's what I call range!

How do birds build nests?

Nests are hard-to-reach hideouts birds make for their eggs and newly hatched chicks. Before building begins, birds scout out the perfect place to set up camp. The best site is one that's safe from sun, wind and rain. Next, they collect the bricks and mortar. In a bird's case, that's twigs and mud. When a bird has about a third of a pound of grass and sticks, it braids them together and cements them with mud. Finally, it uses its tummy to create a cradle in the nest, which it then lines with grass. Home, sweet, home!

FUN FACT! Instead of building their own nests, cuckoo birds lay their eggs in pre-existing ones other birds have created. That's wild!

BLACK-NAPED MONARCH

How many eggs do birds lay at a time?

That depends on the species. Some tropical birds such as toucans lay only two to three eggs each nesting. Wood ducks, on the other hand, lay up to 15!

up to 15

How do eggs hatch?

The babies inside eggs are the main cause. Take soon-to-be-chickens, for example. Chicken eggs hatch about three weeks after they're laid. During an unborn chicken's last week in the egg, its beak and claws become harder and stronger. The birds get bigger, too. By the end of its third week, the bird is big and strong enough to break out of the egg it's so tightly packed into.

DID YOU KNOW?
It's hard to run when you're carrying something heavy, and it's even harder to fly! Like airplanes, birds can't take off if they've got too much cargo on board. A bird's wings wouldn't work with the added weight of a baby, so instead, all 900 species of birds lay eggs.

How fast can horses run?

At full-speed gallop, horses can reach about 35 miles per hour! But they can't keep that pace for more than a couple miles.

35 mph

Do you know the name for a mature male horse?

- **A** Stallion
- **B** Mare
- **C** Foal

Check your answers on page 172!

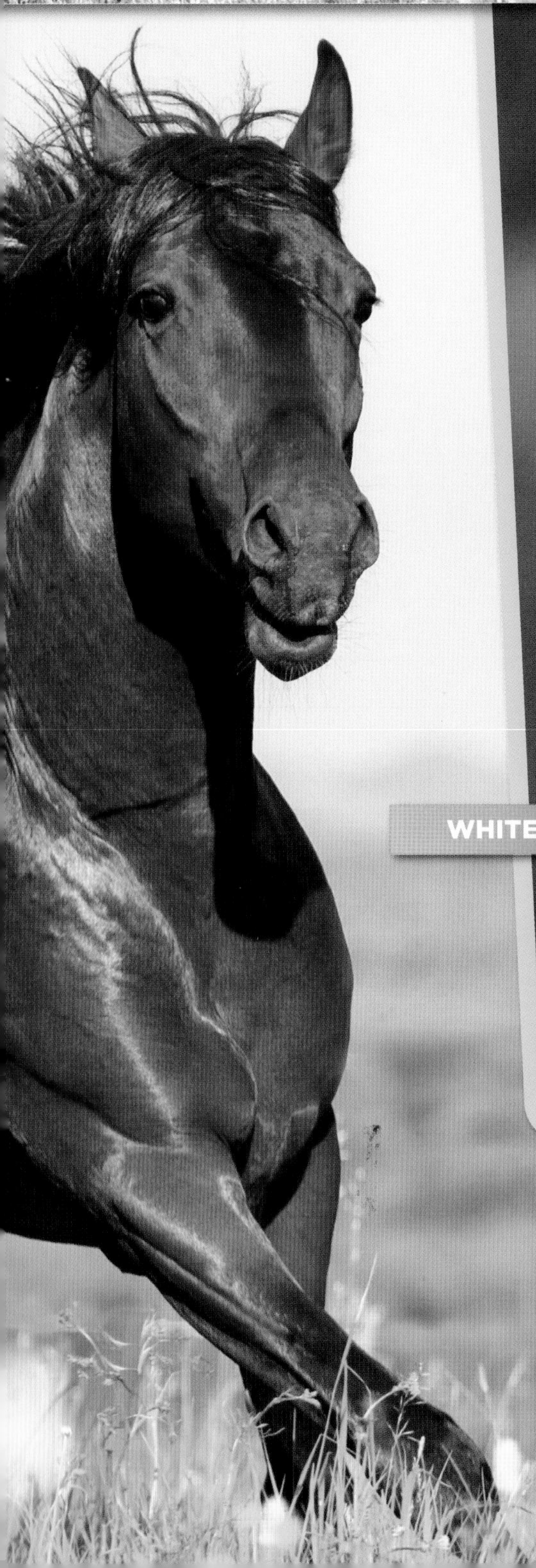

WHITE-TAILED DEER

How quickly do deer antlers grow?

Male deer drop their antlers once a year, but they start growing back almost immediately. The antlers are at their largest in the summer and fall but fall off in the winter. They only take two to four months to grow back, and then the process starts over again!

How do termites eat wood?

Termites have special mouth parts that help them chew wood into little pieces. They also have special bacteria in their guts that help them digest wood better than we could.

DID YOU KNOW?
Termites are the workers that never sleep. Because they stay awake for 24 hours, they can inflict a lot of damage on wood, which you can see to the right!

How do spiders make webs?

Making webs is instinctive for spiders. They were born with the know-how. Spiders have special organs called spinnerets that tell them which type of thread to use. When it wants to begin, a spider will release a silk thread. It anchors the thread someplace—like the corner of your attic or a low-hanging branch. As it moves, it lays more thread, making the web stronger and forming a pattern along the way.

GARDEN SPIDER

How do spiders avoid getting caught in their webs?

Spiders don't come into contact with their webs all at once like their prey do. Instead, they move carefully along the threads and let only the hairs on the tips of their legs touch the sticky parts. They make sure their bodies are clean, too, so they won't get stuck. Another trick some species of spider use is placing "glue" on only some parts of their webs. Other areas, especially where the spider might like to rest, don't have it.

How do caterpillars become butterflies?

Metamorphosis! That's what the process is called. When a caterpillar is fat and long enough, it hangs upside down and covers its body in a silk cocoon. Inside the cocoon, the caterpillar digests itself until only a special set of cells are left. Those cells then divide to form a butterfly. Complicated, I know, but pretty amazing!

FUN FACT! Metamorphosis takes about 10 to 15 days.

LEOPARD LACEWING BUTTERFLY

LEAFCUTTER ANT

How do ants carry things so much bigger than they are?

If ants were our size, they would be much stronger than we are! They have hairs on their feet that stick to smooth surfaces and make gripping the ground easier. They also have large muscles in their heads that close their jaws and help them handle heavy loads. Some ants can carry up to 5,000 times their body weight!

How many ants live in a colony?

Ant colonies come in different shapes and sizes. The smallest are made up of just a few ants, while the biggest, called supercolonies, can have as many as 300 million ants!

DID YOU KNOW?

Ants are extremely social bugs. They live in communities just like humans do. Different ants have different roles. Some ants are workers, which means they build and fix the dirt colony, while others are gatherers. Additionally, each colony has one queen, who rules all of the other ants and keeps order.

How do animals stay warm in the winter?

When animals know cold weather is on its way, some will create burrows under the earth and sleep through the winter. But some animals, like this wood frog, have special chemicals in their blood that keep it from freezing.

WOOD FROG

3 feet per hour

How slow are snails?

Snails are faster than scientists once thought—but they're still pretty slow. They can travel just more than 3 feet per hour.

FUN FACT! Snails have four noses.

How many pet dogs are there in the U.S.?

There are an estimated 70–80 million pet dogs in the United States alone! Sue and I have had many dogs over the years, including Tasha and Brass pictured here, and they were always important members of the family! Having a family pet like a dog, cat or even a hamster can be a great way to learn how to love and nurture—and is also a great way to learn responsibility!

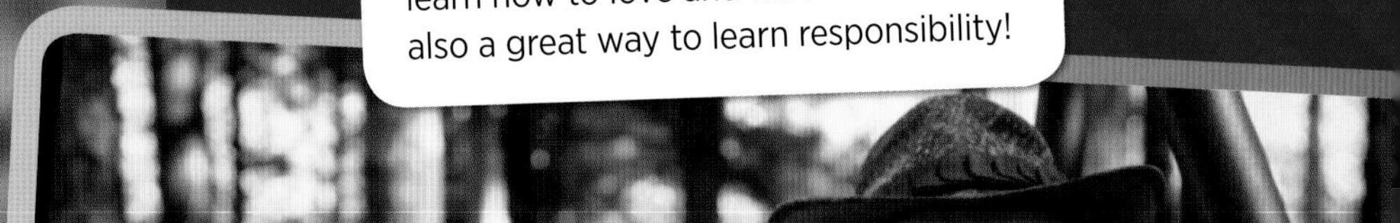

Ah ha ha ha stayin' alive!

How do possums play dead?

In short, they pass out. Possums go limp when they get stressed out or scared. As a predator approaches, possums also secrete a smell that makes the predator believe that it's actually dead. It's a helpful trick that doesn't cause any harm to the possum in the long run.

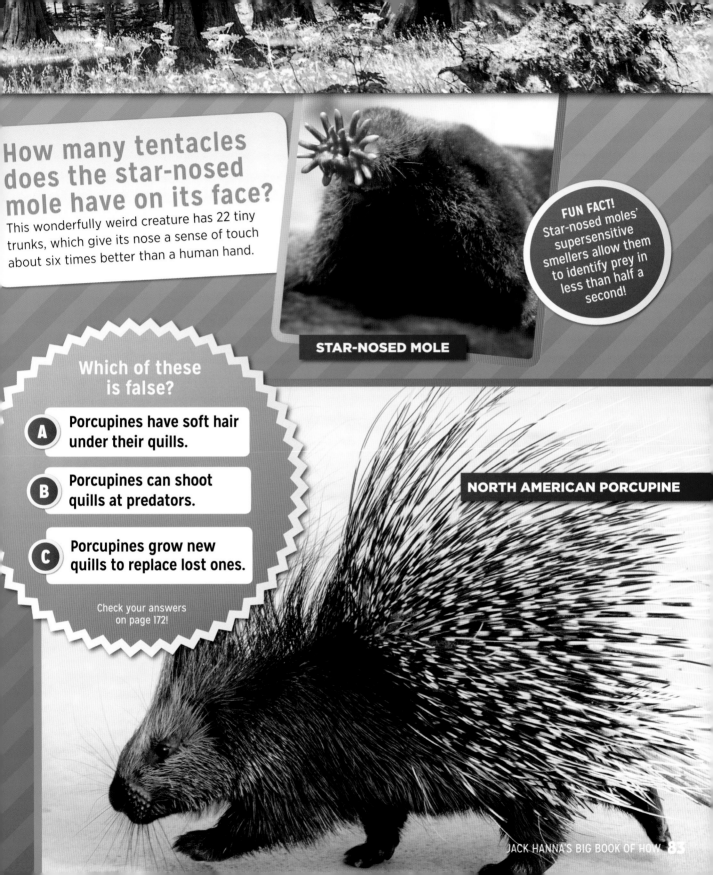

How many tentacles does the star-nosed mole have on its face?

This wonderfully weird creature has 22 tiny trunks, which give its nose a sense of touch about six times better than a human hand.

STAR-NOSED MOLE

FUN FACT!
Star-nosed moles' supersensitive smellers allow them to identify prey in less than half a second!

Which of these is false?

A Porcupines have soft hair under their quills.

B Porcupines can shoot quills at predators.

C Porcupines grow new quills to replace lost ones.

Check your answers on page 172!

NORTH AMERICAN PORCUPINE

How do squirrels find the nuts they hide?

Just like scientists aren't 100 percent sure how human memory works, they haven't quite cracked the squirrel's psyche, either. But researchers know this: Squirrels can remember where they bury nuts. But to err is human—er, squirrel—so they sometimes forget their hiding spots. Luckily, they can smell the stashes, too.

EASTERN GREY SQUIRREL

FUN FACT!
Grey squirrels aren't great at recovering the nuts they bury. They leave 74 percent of them in the ground!

DID YOU KNOW?
Chipmunk cheeks are impressive, but their storage capacity doesn't come close to matching their gathering abilities. A chipmunk can collect as many as 165 acorns in one day. In two days, the animal can gather enough food to last through the entire winter. As you could guess, chipmunks usually hoard a lot more food than they need.

How do ducks float?

They're built for it! Ducks have hollow bones and thick, layered feathers that trap air. Their webbed feet help, too. They allow ducks to swim without wasting energy. Ducks also release special oil that lines their feathers with a waterproof coating.

PUZZLE

This is the most common kind of duck.

LLAARDM

Check your answers on page 172!

FUN FACT!
Most ducklings are born with yellow feathers, but after two months they look like miniature versions of their mother.

GRIZZLY BEAR

How do grizzly bears catch so many fish?

Grizzly bears have a tried-and-true system for eating salmon: They go to the right place at the right time. Once a year, entire schools of salmon swim upstream against the current of a river to spawn. These clever bears have figured this out, so they find a good spot in the water and salmon jump right into their mouths!

FUN FACT!
When it's time for hibernation, Grizzly bears dig their own dens in hillsides.

How do animals know when to hibernate?

Animals hibernate to stay warm when temperatures drop. So cold weather is one reminder! The other has to do with their instincts. Animals who hibernate, including grizzly bears have internal calendars that tell them how to act during each season. Because it's biological, there's no forgetting!

How long do animals hibernate?

That all depends on the animal! Some hibernate for days, while others nap for weeks or even months. Imagine how hungry they must be when they wake up!

Welcome to THE RAINFORE

THESE WET WILDS ARE TEEMING WITH LIFE FROM EVERY CORNER OF THE KINGDOM AND COLOR OF THE RAINBOW

Most tropical rainforests are found right around the equator, an imaginary line that exists halfway between the Earth's top and bottom. Being so close to the equator guarantees it'll always be hot, which rainforests require!

ST

Did you pack your rain boots?

Tropical rainforests are vibrant and damp. They're called rainforests because they receive more than 70 inches of rainfall a year, which is about equal to the height of the average man! All that water helps many types of plants grow, including those dense trees and colorful flowers. Sometimes, it can take a drop of rain 10 minutes to hit the rainforest floor because the tree canopy is so thick! Due to this phenomenon, there are four layers of the rainforest—emergent, canopy, understory and floor—where many different kinds of animals live. Rainforests also can take up a lot of space. The Amazon River Basin forest covers nearly 6 million square miles and takes up 40 percent of the South American country of Brazil. Despite this, rainforests only take up 6 percent of Earth's land. Still, that tiny bit of land is home to more than half the world's wildlife. From toucans to sloths to anteaters, rainforest animals are some of the wildest and wackiest on the planet.

FUN FACT!
The Amazon rainforest is so huge that if it were a nation it would be the ninth largest in the world.

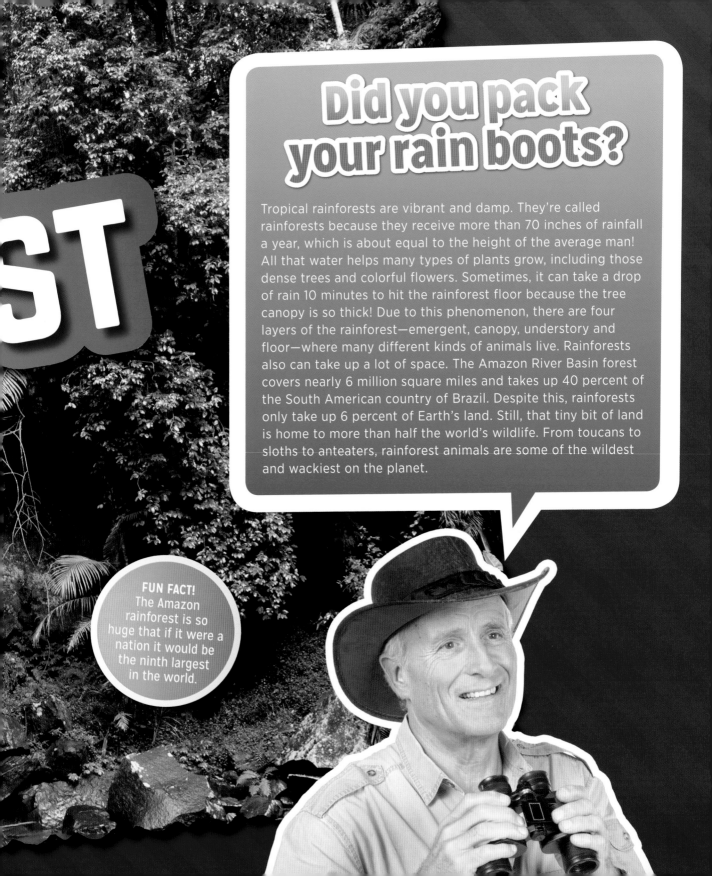

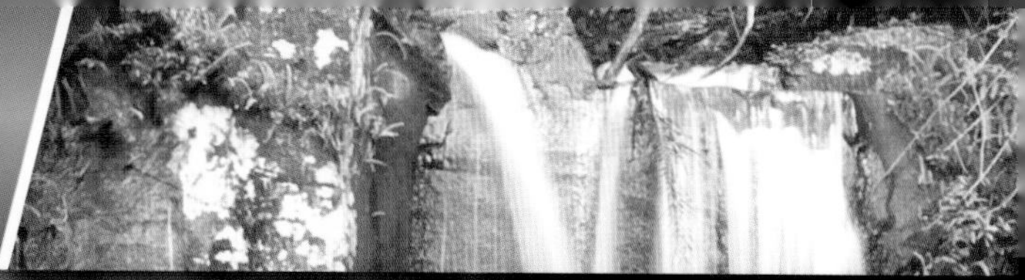

Before this animal becomes a frog, it is a:

- **A** Fish
- **B** Tadpole
- **C** Caterpillar

Check your answers on page 172!

FUN FACT!
If you see a blue poison dart frog, don't touch it! Like their name implies, the skin is poisonous.

BLUE POISON DART FROG

How do small frogs make such loud noises?

Frogs have very simple vocal cords with two slits in the bottom of their mouths that open into what's called a vocal pouch. When air travels from the lungs through the vocal cords, it makes a noise. And when frogs puff themselves up, the noise resonates and becomes even louder! It's difficult for small frogs to make loud noises because it requires a lot more of their energy, but they can still do it!

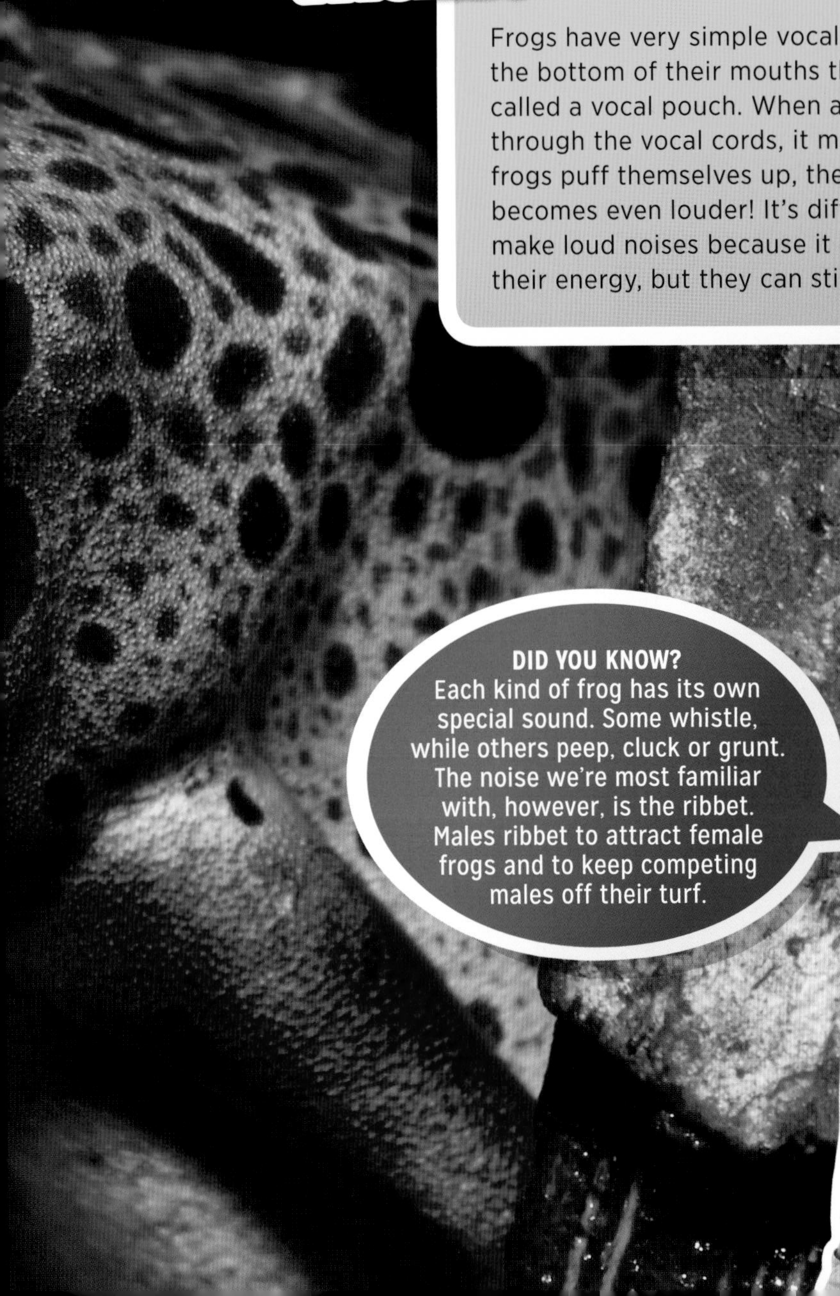

DID YOU KNOW?
Each kind of frog has its own special sound. Some whistle, while others peep, cluck or grunt. The noise we're most familiar with, however, is the ribbet. Males ribbet to attract female frogs and to keep competing males off their turf.

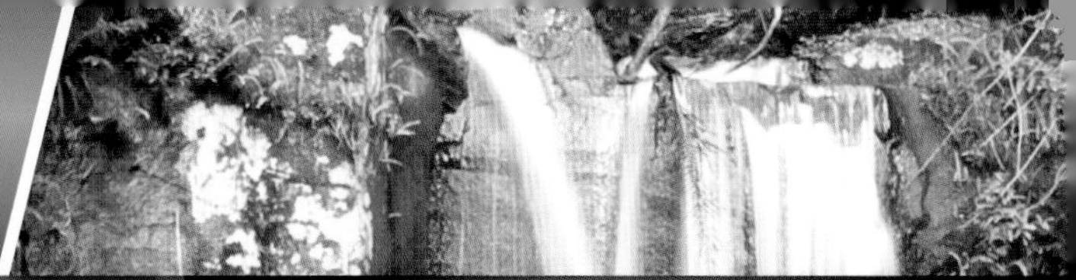

How do parrots talk?

In truth, parrots can't "talk." But they do mimic. Parrots don't know what they're saying, but they're awfully good at saying it! Parrots can imitate what they've heard because their brains are structured differently than the brains of other birds. For example, parrots can only say "Paige want a cracker," if they've heard it before. But they can't answer questions like "What would you like for dinner?" or strike up a conversation. Parrots have "cores" in their brains that control vocal learning—most other animals don't have these cores, so they can't execute the trick.

FUN FACT! Macaws and cockatoos have been known to live for 50 years!

AFRICAN GREY PARROT

SCARLET MACAW AND BLUE AND YELLOW MACAW

How are parrots and macaws different?

Macaws are a specific type of parrot, but there are lots of other types, too. For example, parakeets are also parrots. If you're confused, think about it this way: All squares are rectangles, but not all rectangles are squares. That's how it works for parrots and macaws, too. All macaws are parrots, but not all parrots are macaws.

BLUE-FRONTED AMAZON

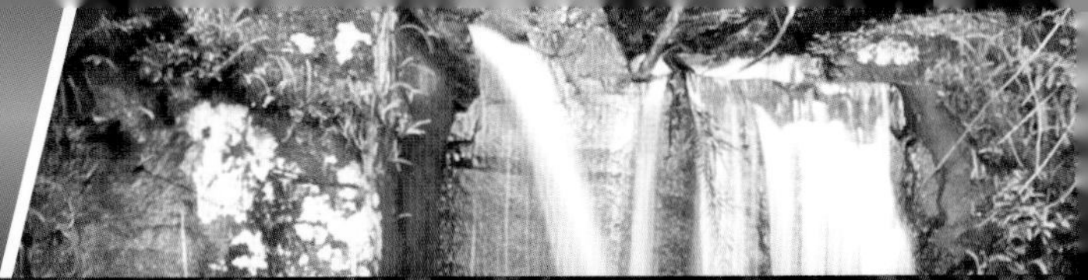

How do peacocks use their feathers?

Peacocks use their feathers to make themselves look more attractive! In the animal world, males are often the ones facing the pressure to look good for their mates, and a male peacock's plumage is his greatest asset when seeking to catch a peahen's eye.

PUZZLE

Peafowl are the national bird of this country.

DIINA

Check your answers on page 172!

Hello, ladies!

FUN FACT! Female peafowl are called peahens.

How long are snakes?

Just like people, snakes differ in size. But snakes vary in size much more drastically than humans! The smallest known snake is less than 4 inches long. The longest snake on record is a python named Medusa, who measured 25 feet 2 inches!

GREEN TREE PYTHON

FUN FACT! Pythons have fangs, but they don't produce venom!

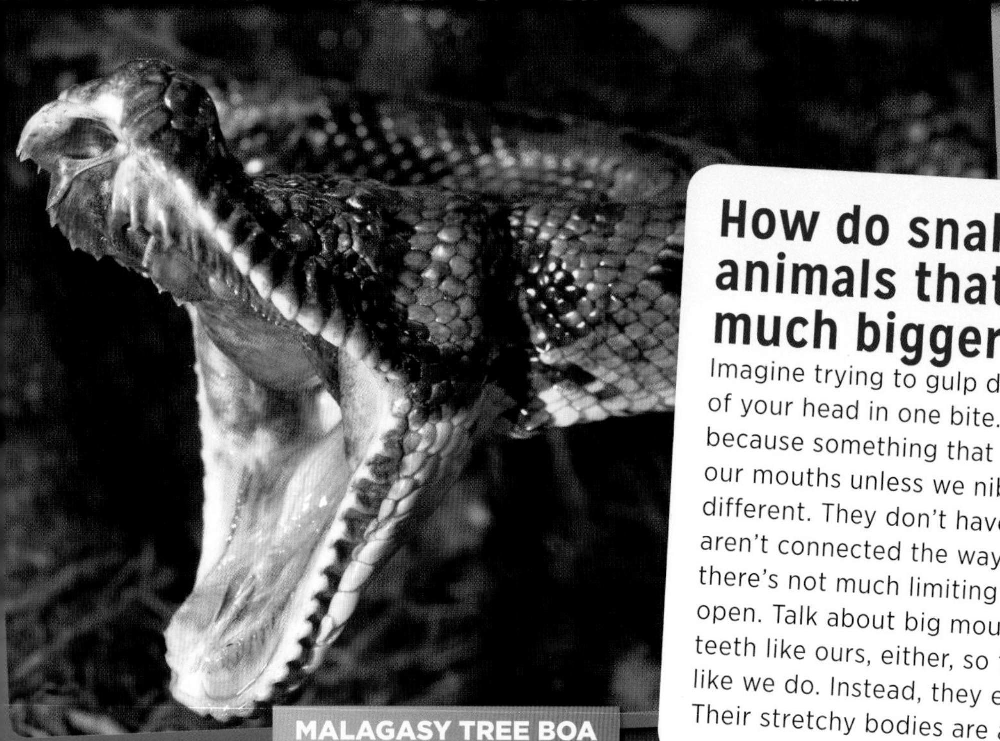

MALAGASY TREE BOA

How do snakes eat animals that are so much bigger than them?

Imagine trying to gulp down a cookie the size of your head in one bite. It's hard to picture because something that large wouldn't fit in our mouths unless we nibbled at it. Snakes are different. They don't have chins, so their jaws aren't connected the way ours are. That means there's not much limiting how wide their jaws open. Talk about big mouths! Snakes don't have teeth like ours, either, so they can't chew food like we do. Instead, they eat meals in one go. Their stretchy bodies are a big help, too.

How do snakes have babies?

You're probably wondering whether snakes lay eggs or give birth to live animals. The answer is both! It all depends on the species. For example, Burmese pythons lay eggs, while boa constrictors have live babies. Some species do a combination of both! Rattlesnakes lay eggs inside their bodies that stay there until the eggs hatch.

BURMESE PYTHON

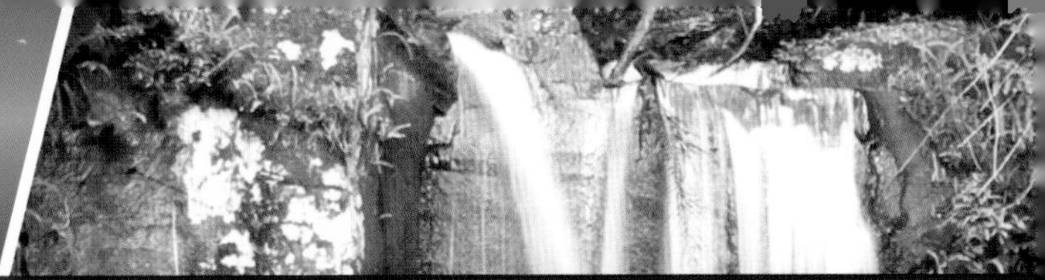

How long are frogs' tongues?

A frog's tongue is about ⅓ the length of its body! If your tongue was that long, it could probably reach your belly button!

AMERICAN GREEN TREE FROG

How do frogs catch flies with their tongues?

Frogs have long, sticky tongues that make catching prey easier. The tackiness works like the glue on Post-It notes. When they spot a snack, they quickly shoot their tongues out and use the natural glue to nab their prey.

How are insects and bugs different?

What scientists call "true bugs" have straws for mouths and suck up their food—like ants. Certain kinds of insects don't. All bugs are considered insects. But most people, except for scientists, use the words bugs and insects interchangeably.

FUN FACT!
Certain species of frog can lift meals three times heavier than their body weight!

How many insects are there in the world?

Insects are the most diverse, plentiful organisms in the world! About 900,000 different kinds have been discovered, and scientists think there are even more out there. Researchers believe that at any given time there are about 10 quintillion insects alive! That's

10,000,000,000,000,000,000!

How much blood do bats drink?

Only one type of bat—the vampire bat—drinks blood, but its thirst is extreme. A colony of 100 bats can drain all the blood from 25 cows in just one year's time!

VAMPIRE BAT

How slow are sloths?

Really, really, really slow—sloths only move about 125 feet per day. Even their bodies process food slowly! It can take up to a month for food to pass through a sloth's digestive system.

FUN FACT!
Cows moo, dogs bark and sloths... sound like deflating balloons. If need be, they can squeal or grunt, too.

Do I have something on my nose? I'll get it. Next month.

How do sloths protect themselves?

When in danger, sloths can move faster and farther than usual, but it wears them out big time! When predators such as jaguars, harpy eagles or anacondas attack, sloths use their sharp claws and teeth to defend themselves. Then, they'll flee through the forest treetops.

How much do sloths sleep?

About 20 hours per day! That means they're only awake for about four. And you thought you were sleepy!

DID YOU KNOW?
Sloths are strong swimmers! Their long arms are very useful in the water.

How are monkeys and apes different?

A lot of people use the words "monkey" and "ape" interchangeably, but the animals are different. Sure, they're both primates, but apes have bigger bodies and brains than monkeys. Another difference is that monkeys have tails, but apes usually don't. There are exceptions to every rule, however. For example, some monkeys are big and don't have tails. Similarly, some apes, like gibbons, are smaller than certain monkeys.

How are apes related to people?

Apes are our closest relatives in the animal kingdom. In fact, we share as much as 95 percent of our genes (the stuff inside us that makes us look and act the way we do) with them. Millions of years ago, we even shared an ancestor!

WESTERN LOWLAND GORILLA

PUZZLE

This type of ape is the largest primate.

AGROLLI

Check your answers on page 172!

It is always amazing to see mountain gorillas in Rwanda. We saw this pair in 2011.

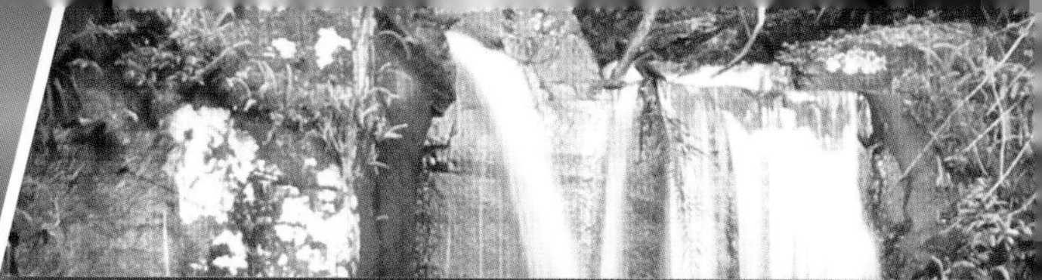

You eyeballin' me?

FUN FACT!
Chameleons see double—literally! By rotating and focusing both eyes on two things at once, the lizard can see what's on either side of its body at the same time!

PANTHER CHAMELEON

How do chameleons change color?

In most creatures, pigment (the stuff that gives things color) lives in little sacks within cells. But chameleons are different. Their pigment is stored in cells that can expand and contract. So when a chameleon is excited, its cells with red pigment might expand, while other colored cells might contract. That's a simplified version of how they do it!

DID YOU KNOW?
The idea that chameleons change color to blend into their surroundings is a myth, but they do have other tricks up their sleeves! Tree-dwelling chameleons can narrow their bodies so they are thin enough to hide behind branches, while ground chameleons can lay down and contort their bodies so they look like crumpled leaves.

How do toucans use their beaks?

These tropical birds use their beaks to grab and peel the fruit they eat. But toucans also use their beaks like a thermostat. The blood vessels packed in their beaks keep them cool on hot days and warm in cooler weather!

How do birds fly in the rain?

Birds create special water-resistant oil they rub on their feathers when it rains. The layer of protection makes flying in the rain manageable—but not enjoyable—for select species.

WHITE-NECKED JACOBIN

FUN FACT! Hummingbirds aren't bothered by rain. In fact, they're great at flying in it!

How high do birds fly?

Birds typically fly as high as 500 feet, which is about half the height of the Eiffel Tower. When they migrate, however, flocks of birds can soar thousands of feet in the air!

How many different kinds of birds exist?

More than 10,000—and those are the ones we know about! Scientists are discovering new birds all the time.

How many ants do anteaters eat?

Giant anteaters can slurp down as many as 30,000 ants each day! Yum!

Can you guess how much more powerful an anteater's sense of smell is than a human's?

- **A** 10 times
- **B** 25 times
- **C** 40 times

Check your answers on page 172!

FUN FACT!
Anteaters aren't immune to ant bites, so they don't stay at a hill long before moving on.

DID YOU KNOW?
While anteaters primarily eat ants, they are capable of digesting other things! An anteater won't turn its snout up at ripe fruit it finds on the ground.

BLACK PANTHER

FUN FACT!
If you look closely at melanistic leopards, you can see they still have spots just like other leopards, despite their dark fur.

How are panthers different from leopards?

Black panthers, also called melanistic leopards, are a special kind of leopard. Being melanistic means the leopards have lots of extra black pigment. That accounts for the animal's color.

MEXICAN SPIDER MONKEY

How do monkeys hang from their tails?

Animals' tails have a number of uses, from helping with balance, swatting bugs or even as a way to communicate (as any owner of a happy dog can attest). Monkeys have prehensile tails, which means they're capable of grasping things. Because of this, a monkey can use his tail like an extra limb! Wouldn't that be nice? Think of all the extra stuff you could grab!

FUN FACT!
Not all rainforest animals are bright and colorful! Take the harpy eagle, for example. They're shades of gray.

STRAWBERRY POISON-DART FROG

How do colorful animals disguise themselves?

Filled with lush vegetation and vibrant flowers, the rainforest itself is as colorful as a pack of crayons. The animals that live there have adapted accordingly. From blue macaws to orange poisonous dart frogs, rainforest animals use their patterns to blend into their surroundings. Monkeys natch tree bark, big dark cats blend into the hadows and colorful birds match the fruit and ne flowers that fill the trees. In the rainforest, nimals with bold, rainbow patterns blend right in.

How are crocodiles and alligators different?

Crocodiles and alligators are reptiles that might look the same, but they are very different. Crocodiles are grayish green with a V-shaped snout. Alligators, on the other hand, are black with U-shaped snouts. Also, crocodiles still have a toothy grin when their mouths are shut, but you can't see alligators's teeth at all. Another thing to note is that crocodiles swim in saltwater, while alligators prefer freshwater.

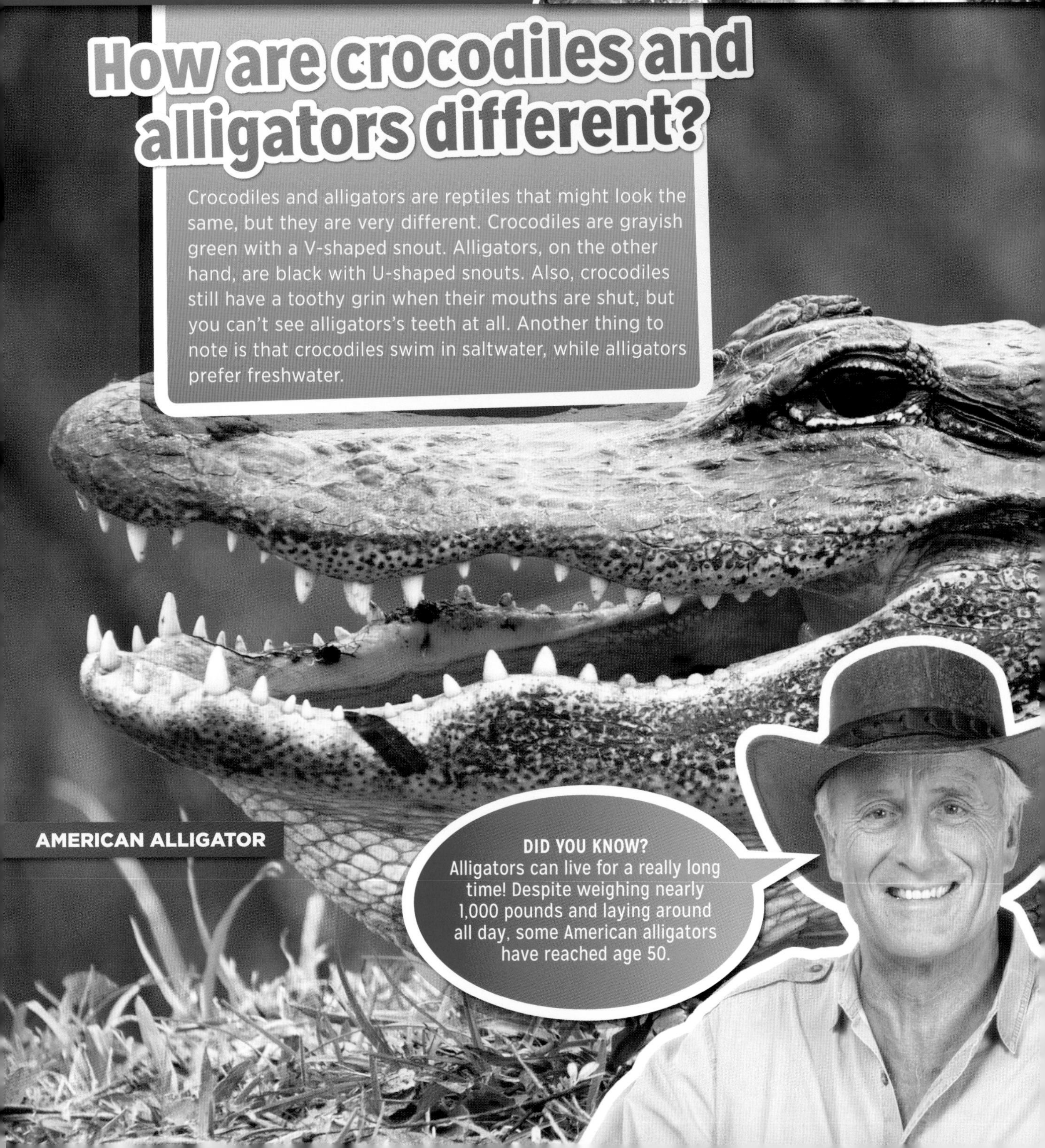

AMERICAN ALLIGATOR

DID YOU KNOW?
Alligators can live for a really long time! Despite weighing nearly 1,000 pounds and laying around all day, some American alligators have reached age 50.

Like crocodiles, alligators and frogs, humans belong to this kingdom:

- **A** Animal
- **B** Plant
- **C** Fungi

Check your answers on page 172!

How do tadpoles turn into frogs?

Like caterpillars turn into butterflies, tadpoles undergo metamorphosis to become frogs. Unlike caterpillars, tadpoles don't have to wrap themselves in cocoons to change shape. Instead, it's programmed into their genes, just like humans are programmed to grow taller. It's pretty much automatic!

FUN FACT! Frogs shed their skin about once a week. Afterward, they usually eat it!

COMMON TOAD

How do toads protect themselves from predators?

Toads have a lot of different defense mechanisms. Most impressively, their warts are filled with poison that's very off-putting to animals who might look at a toad and see a tasty snack. If that wasn't enough, their body coloring helps them to blend in with their environment, and they can also puff up to make themselves appear too large for predators to eat. And if all else fails, a toad might even play dead!

GIANT PANDA

Can't talk. Eating.

Can you guess which body part pandas have that other bears don't?

- **A** Thumbs
- **B** Tails
- **C** Ears

Check your answers on page 172!

FUN FACT!
At birth, a panda bear is smaller than a grown mouse!

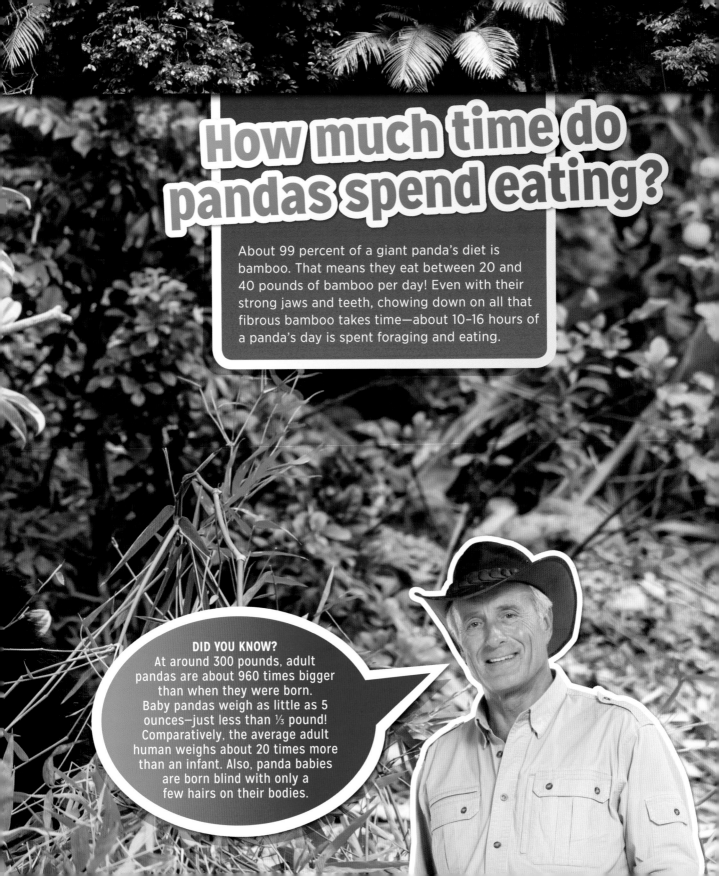

How much time do pandas spend eating?

About 99 percent of a giant panda's diet is bamboo. That means they eat between 20 and 40 pounds of bamboo per day! Even with their strong jaws and teeth, chowing down on all that fibrous bamboo takes time—about 10–16 hours of a panda's day is spent foraging and eating.

DID YOU KNOW?
At around 300 pounds, adult pandas are about 960 times bigger than when they were born. Baby pandas weigh as little as 5 ounces—just less than ⅓ pound! Comparatively, the average adult human weighs about 20 times more than an infant. Also, panda babies are born blind with only a few hairs on their bodies.

How do animals become endangered?

Animals can become endangered for numerous reasons including habitat loss, spread of disease or poaching.

DYEING POISON DART FROG

SOUND IT OUT!

endangered
(en - DAYN - jerd)

Endangered means at risk of extinction. When an animal goes extinct, there are none left in the world. For example, dinosaurs are extinct.

DID YOU KNOW?
This vibrant poison dart frog is critically endangered because their habitat is being destroyed. But you can do lots of little things to help endangered animals like the poison dart frog! Recycling and using less water both help. So does respecting the environment by remembering not to litter!

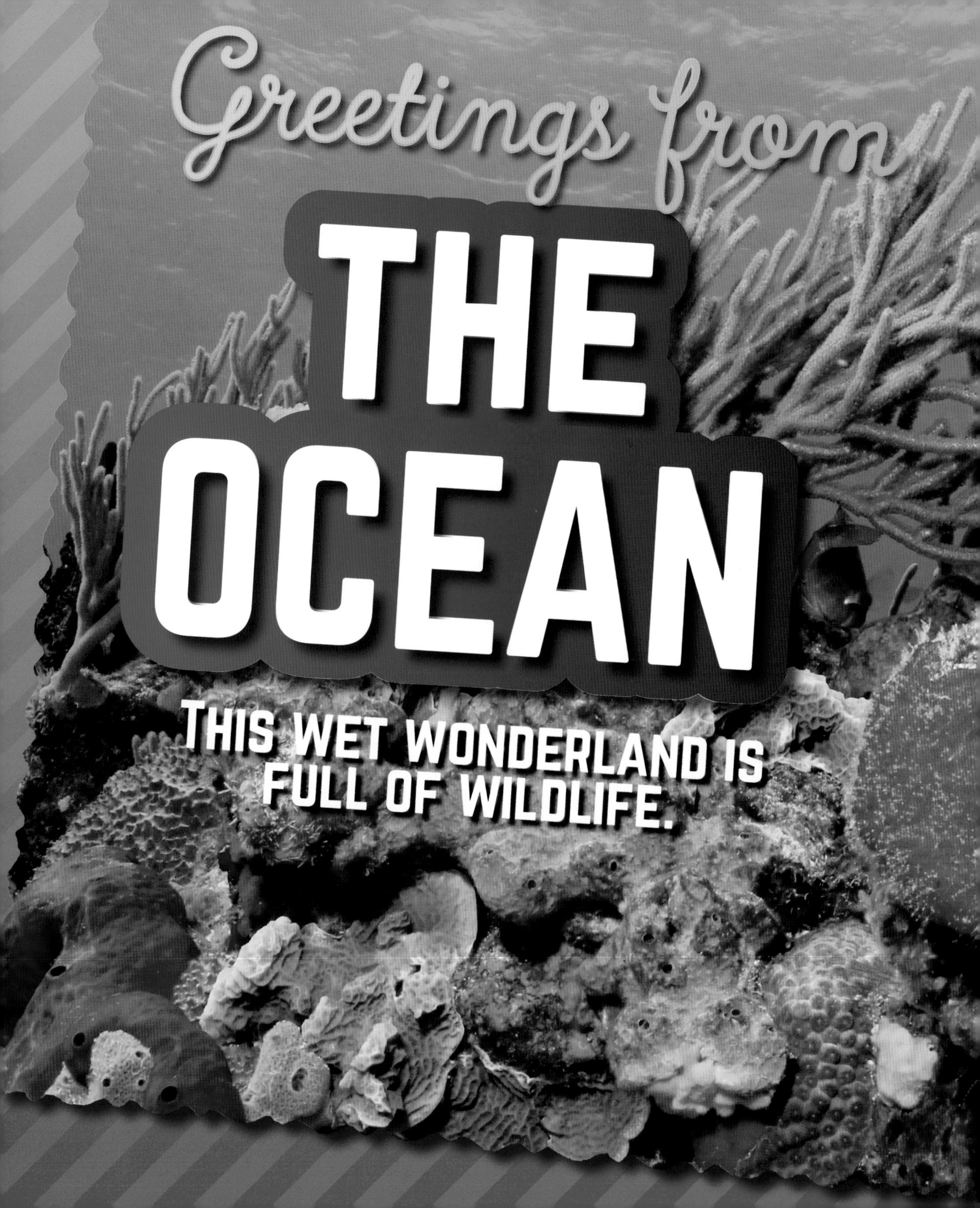

Greetings from THE OCEAN

THIS WET WONDERLAND IS FULL OF WILDLIFE.

FUN FACT!
The world's coral reefs first formed around 500 million years ago.

Hope you brought goggles!

The ocean is the world's largest habitat. It takes up 71 percent of the Earth. There are three major oceans—the Pacific, the Atlantic and the Indian. Even though the oceans are different temperatures with different currents, they all touch. More than one million different kinds of animals live in the 320 million cubic miles of water that make up the ocean. From the mysterious marine life that swims in the deepest, darkest parts of the sea to the social fish that nip at the water's surface, interesting animals fill every inch of the ocean!

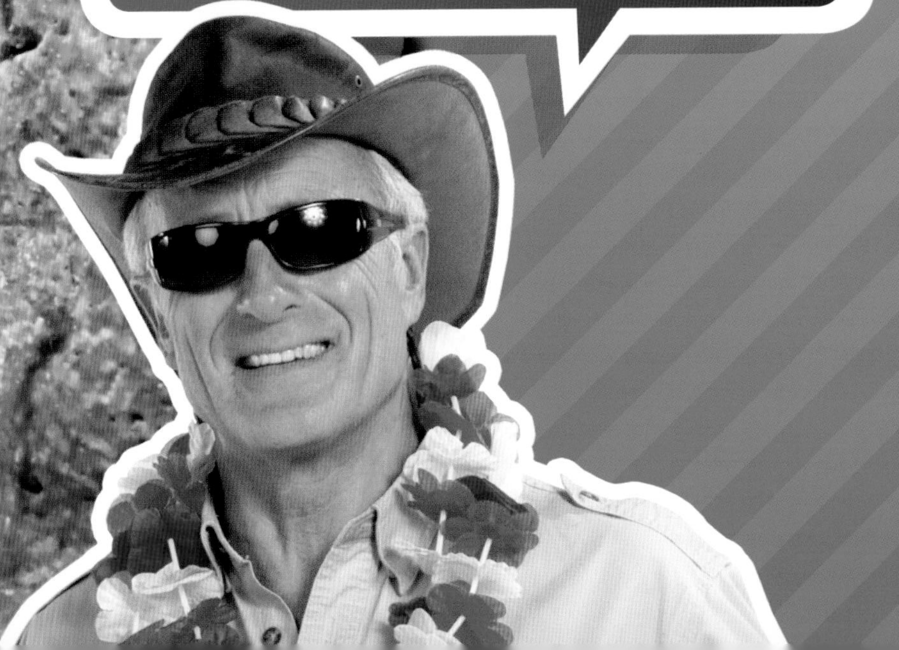

HUMPBACK WHALES

How do whales use their blowholes?

Whales (and dolphins, too) don't breathe water through gills like their fish neighbors can. Instead, these aquatic mammals have lungs just like humans! Whales fill up their lungs with air by breathing through their blowholes above water, just like you'd use your nose or mouth to breathe before diving in a swimming pool.

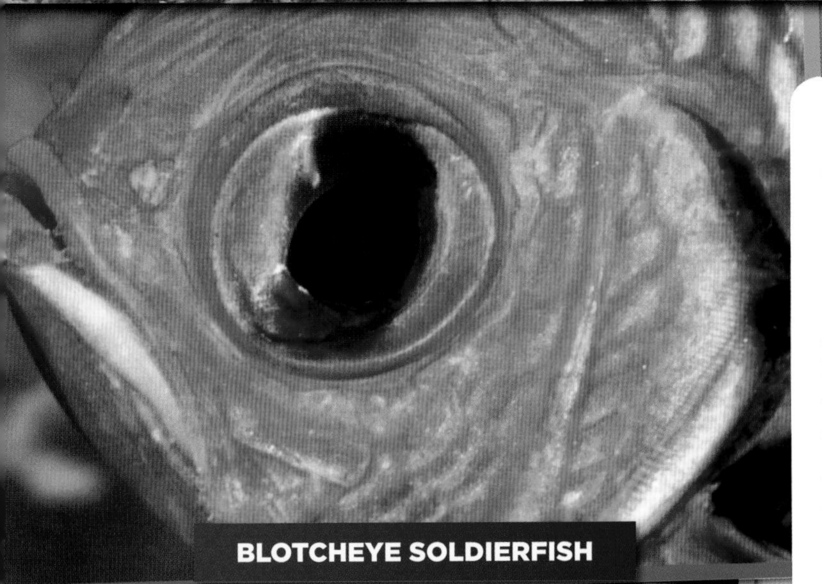

BLOTCHEYE SOLDIERFISH

How can fish keep their eyes open underwater for so long?

Just like fish can breathe water and land animals can't, fish are equipped with eyes that have adapted to see in water from the moment they're born. Just like your eyes have evolved to be comfortable in air, fish have evolved eyes that are perfectly at home in the ocean.

LIONFISH

How do fish survive without oxygen?

They don't have to! All fish need oxygen just like humans do, they just get it in a different way. Using their gills, fish send oxygen directly to their bloodstreams and get rid of all the extra water. Basically, they just drink instead of breathe! But if the water they're swimming in doesn't have enough oxygen to keep the fish alive, they can drown just like mammals.

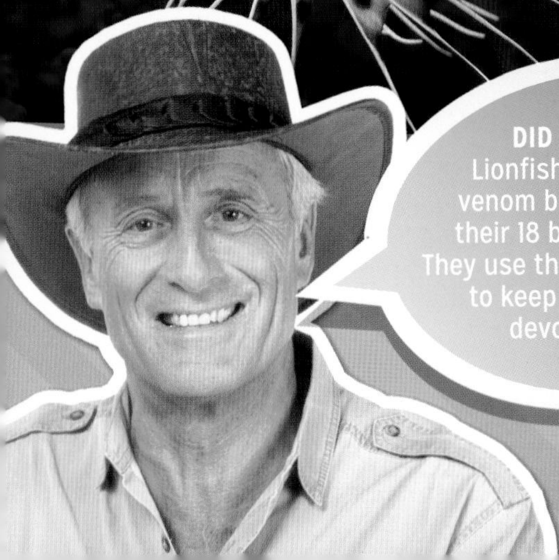

DID YOU KNOW?
Lionfish have a painful venom built in to each of their 18 back (dorsal) fins. They use the poisonous pokers to keep predators from devouring them.

How big are whales?

Whales come in different shapes and sizes, but blue whales are the biggest of them all. They hold the title of largest animal on Earth, too. They can reach up to 200 tons and 105 feet, with tongues as heavy as elephants and hearts as large as cars! Even smaller whales such as the beluga are sizeable. They can reach up to 3,000 pounds and 20 feet.

FUN FACT!
Sperm whales have the world's heaviest brains!

HUMPBACK WHALE

How do whales sing?

Most whales make noise by passing air through their sinuses, which can sound like singing. But scientists think certain kinds, such as humpbacks, have vocal chords like humans! The jury's still out on that one, but researchers can agree on this: Only male humpbacks are doing the singing.

How much do whales eat?

Tons! Literally. Blue whales can eat about four tons of krill in a day during certain seasons. Belugas eat less—about 55 pounds per day. But that's still a big meal!

PUZZLE

Whales breathe through these.

B H O O L E S L W

Check your answers on page 172!

How fast can dolphins swim?

Scientists haven't studied the speed of every kind of dolphin. (There are more than 30 different species!) What scientists do know is how fast the bottlenose dolphin travels: 3 to 7 miles per hour on average. When they're working hard, they can reach speeds of more than 20 miles per hour!

How do dolphins stay underwater for so long?

Dolphins slow their heart rate and stop their breathing while underwater. They also have a special protein in their muscles that helps them store tons of air there.

SPINNER DOLPHINS

FUN FACT!
Unlike humans, dolphins can move their left and right eyes separately. This means they can be looking to the left with their left eye, while their right eye looks straight ahead.

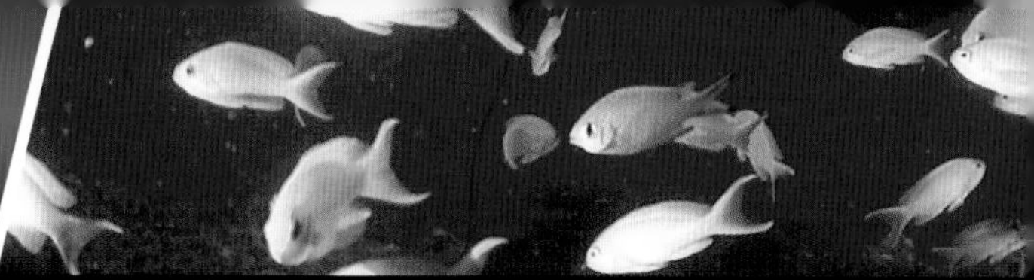

How are whales and sharks different?

Lots of people wrongly think sharks and whales are alike. It's an easy mistake to make with names like "whale shark" floating around. But the two animals are very different! First of all, sharks are fish, and whales are mammals. That means sharks have gills, while whales breathe with their lungs. Unlike whales, who have bone skeletons, sharks' are made of cartilage—the stuff our ears and noses are made of. Sharks don't have a single bone in their bodies!

WHALE SHARK

DID YOU KNOW?
The whale shark is the largest shark. They're even bigger than great white sharks! They can grow as long as a school bus and weigh as much as 40,000 pounds. The smallest shark that we know about is the dwarf lanternshark, which is about six and a half inches long!

How many different kinds of sharks are there?

There are more than 400 different shark species.

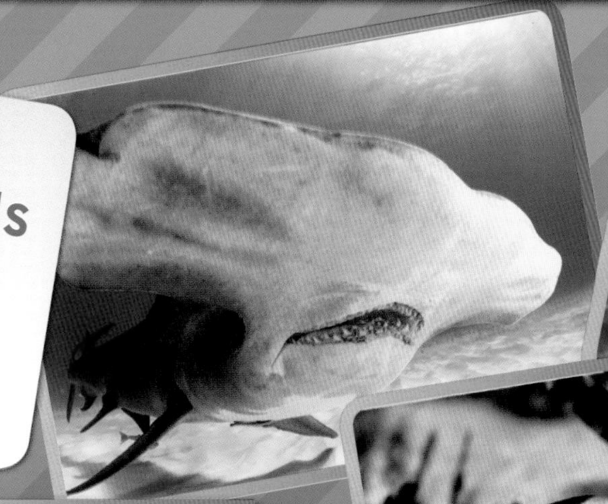

HAMMERHEAD SHARK

CARPET SHARK

BROWNBANDED BAMBOO SHARK

FUN FACT!
Killer whales aren't whales at all! They're actually a type of dolphin.

How many orcas live together in a "pod?"

Orcas are extremely social animals that live in groups called pods of up to 30 individuals, but pods have been known to combine to form larger groups of up to 100. Killer whales, as orcas are sometimes known despite being more closely related to dolphins, use these numbers—along with their big brains—to come up with hunting strategies and coordinate attacks on seals and other animals.

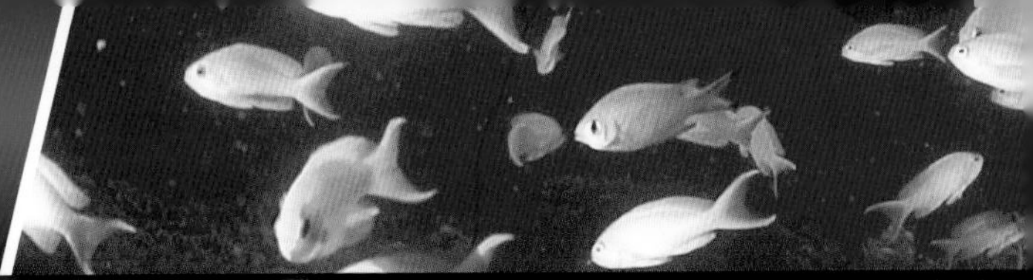

How many teeth do sharks have?

Sharks never stop growing new teeth, and some species have as many as eight rows. In a lifetime, a shark could have up to 50,000 teeth—but not all at once.

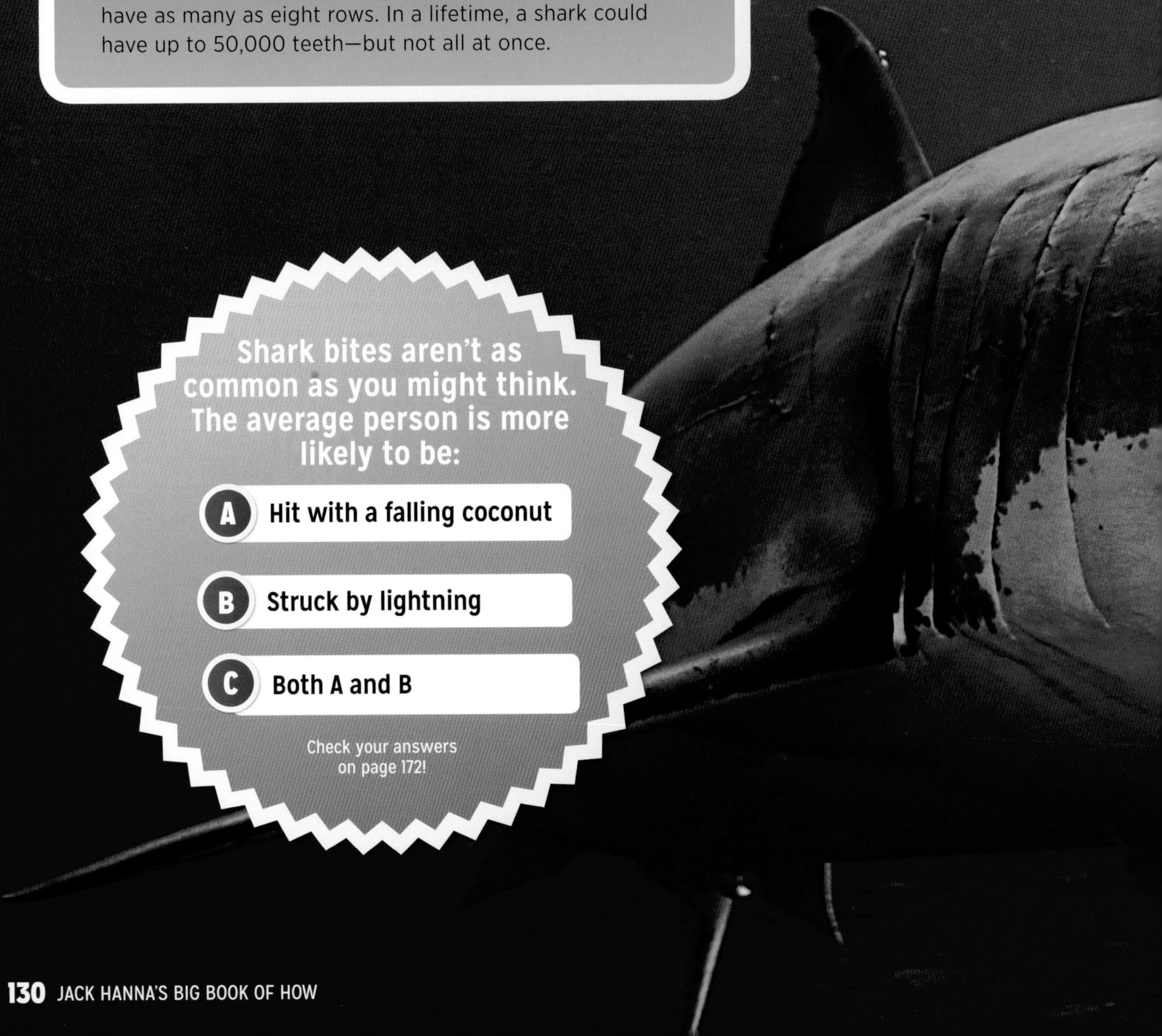

Shark bites aren't as common as you might think. The average person is more likely to be:

- **A** Hit with a falling coconut
- **B** Struck by lightning
- **C** Both A and B

Check your answers on page 172!

GREAT WHITE SHARK

FUN FACT!
Sharks use their teeth to rip, not to chew. They swallow chunks of food whole.

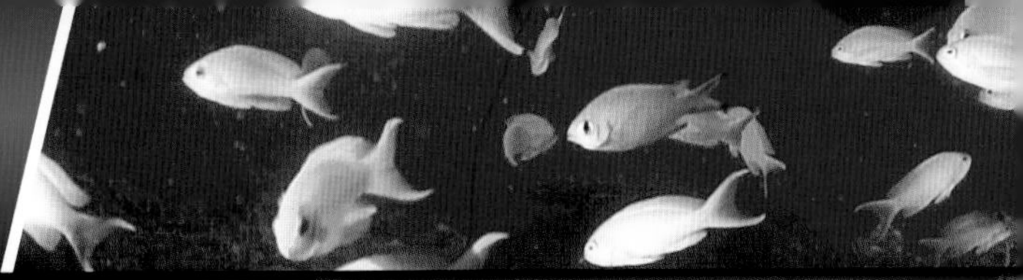

How old is the jellyfish species?

Jellyfish have been around for at least 500 million years! They were swimming through the oceans even before dinosaurs existed.

How much do jellyfish weigh?

Although they look like floating bags of air, jellyfish are heavier than you might expect. Smaller jellyfish, such as the Box jellyfish, weigh up to 4.4 pounds!

FUN FACT!
Jellyfish don't have hearts, bones, blood or brains! But they do have nerves, which help them sense things.

How do jellyfish sting?

Like snakes, jellyfish are venomous. They have tiny stinging cells in their tentacles that stun or paralyze anything they touch. If jellyfish feel threatened, they'll throw out a tentacle to protect themselves.

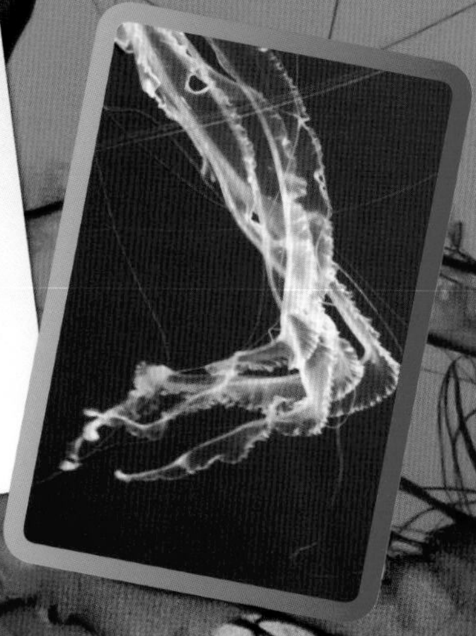

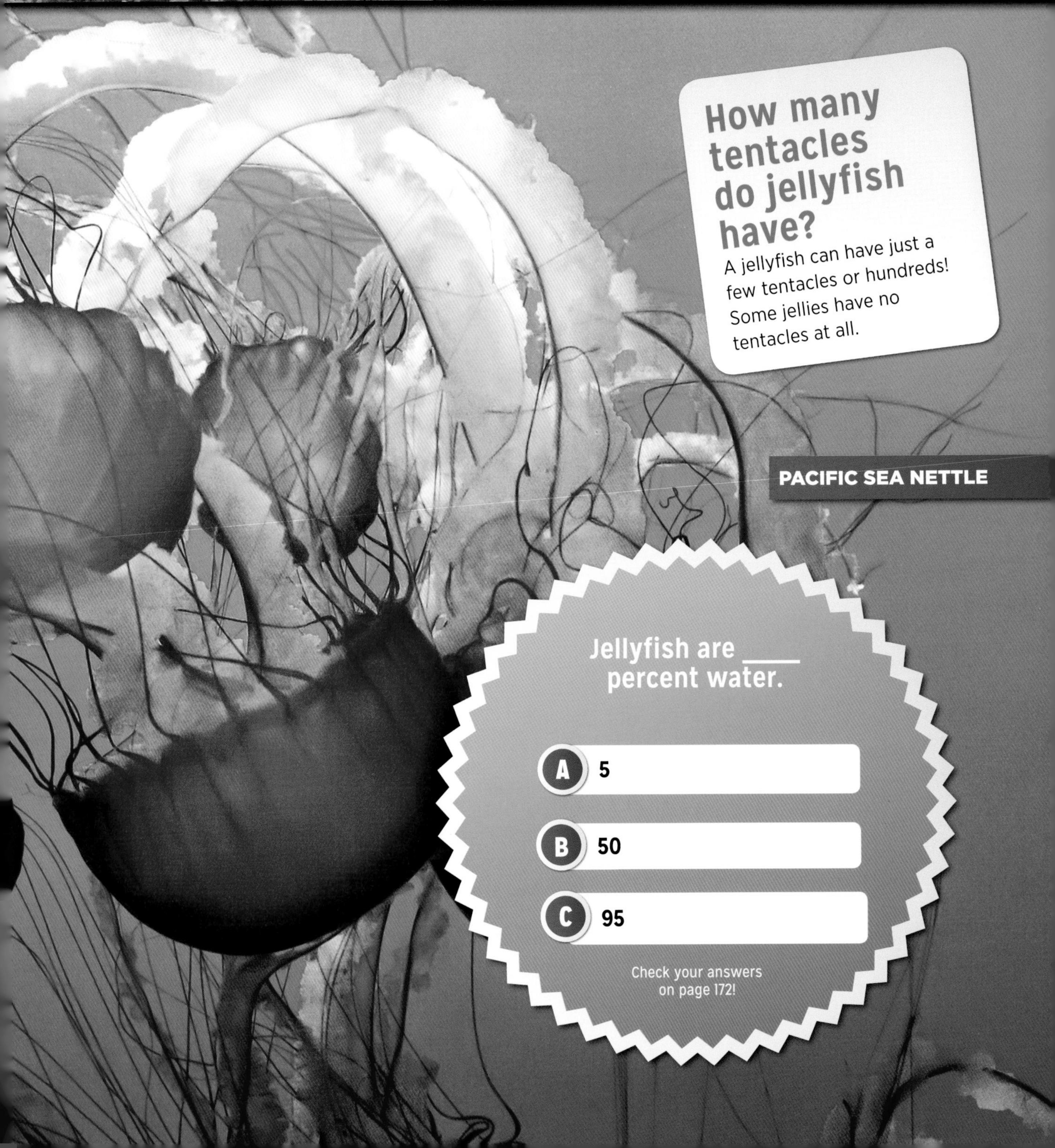

How many tentacles do jellyfish have?

A jellyfish can have just a few tentacles or hundreds! Some jellies have no tentacles at all.

PACIFIC SEA NETTLE

Jellyfish are ____ percent water.

- A 5
- B 50
- C 95

Check your answers on page 172!

How fast are jellyfish?

The average speed of a jellyfish is five miles per hour, which is faster than the average human adult's walking pace! Humans generally walk a single mile in around 15 minutes, giving us a speed of about four miles per hour. But jellyfish mostly rely on the ocean current to carry them around the ocean, which is one reason why you'll see jellyfish traveling in blooms—they usually float together!

FUN FACT! Most fish have taste buds all over their bodies!

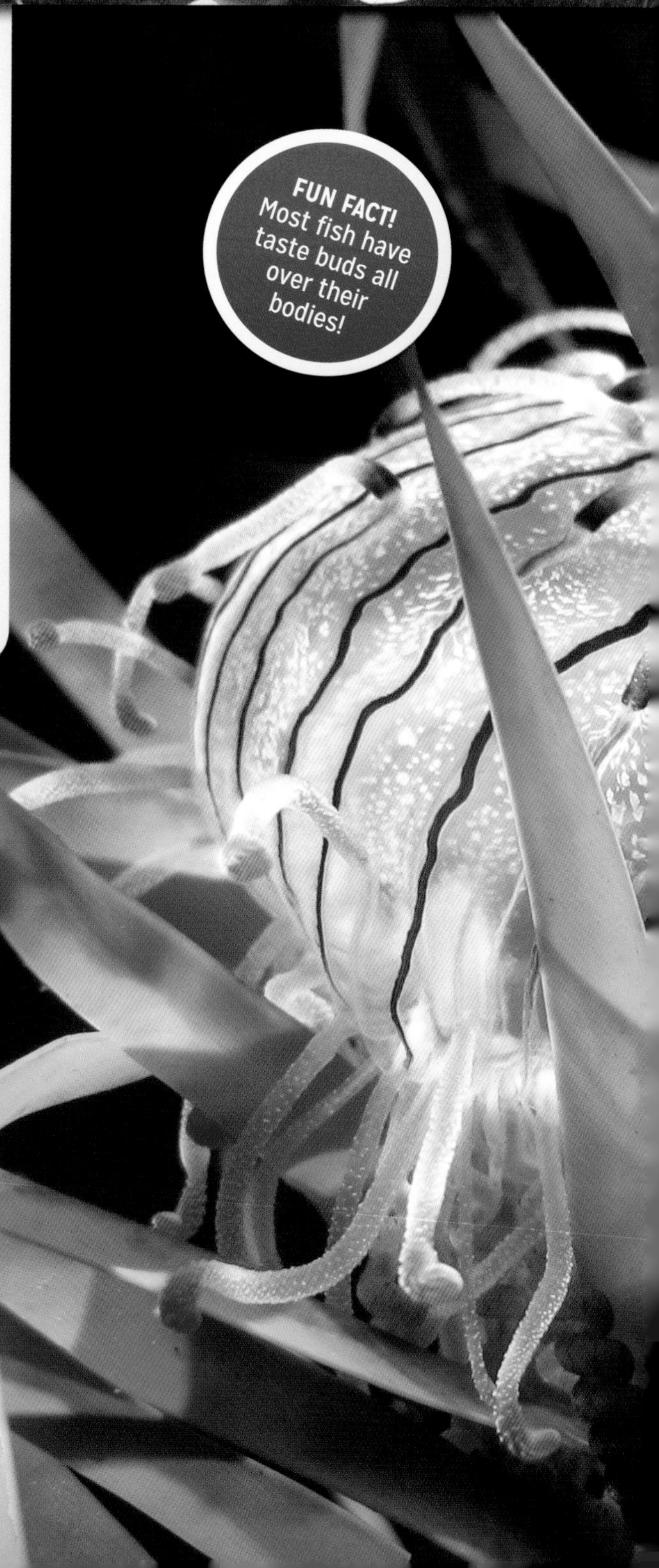

MOON JELLYFISH

How do jellyfish swim?

When a jellyfish swims, it looks like it's using its many tentacles to swim forward. This actually isn't the case! Jellyfish propel themselves through the water by acting a little like a vacuum cleaner. By sucking in water, they're able to swim by pulling themselves forward.

FLOWER HAT JELLYFISH

How do fish stay afloat when they sleep?

The way fish sleep is different from the way mammals sleep. Scientists are still doing research on fish's sleep habits, but they've figured out that fish do rest—with their eyes open! When they want to sleep, some fish go hide near rocks or coral near the ocean floor, occasionally moving their fins to keep swimming.

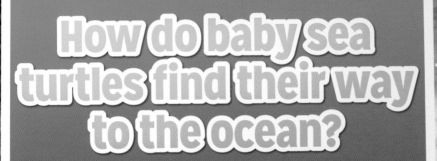

How do baby sea turtles find their way to the ocean?

It's an instinct like bird migration. The babies automatically know they should do it. Once the turtles are born on land, they follow the light of the moon and slight differences in the Earth's magnetic field and head for the water.

PUZZLE

Turtles can't stick these out!

S T O N U E G

Check your answers on page 172!

FUN FACT!
Olive ridley sea turtles migrate hundreds of miles to lay eggs. After Monterey Bay Aquarium let a turtle go, they found it had traveled from San Diego to Mazatlán, Mexico!

OLIVE RIDLEY SEA TURTLE

How do eels create electricity?

Eels have special nerves that act like a battery. The eel's brain just needs to tell the nerves to shock something, and it'll create electricity.

ELECTRIC EEL

FUN FACT!
An electric eel's vital organs only take up 20 percent of its body. The rest is comprised of the cells that allow it to zap its prey at up to 600 volts.

I'm electric! Boogie woogie woogie!

How do oysters make pearls?

Oysters only make pearls when a grain of sand somehow gets inside its shell. The oyster worries that the sand will irritate its skin and protects itself by covering the grain of sand with mother-of-pearl, the substance that forms the inner layer of an oyster's shell, until it becomes a pearl. Sand might not be worth much, but a pearl sure is!

How are clams and oysters different?

Clams are round and semi-smooth, while oysters are rough and long. Another difference is that clams can move around, but oysters are stuck in one spot for most of their lives!

PACIFIC OYSTER

EUROPEAN FLAT OYSTER

How do shelled animals grow?

Hermit crabs grow like people do, but the difference is that they molt. That just means they shed their shells in search of bigger ones.

HERMIT CRAB

How do coral reefs form?

Coral reefs form when coral larvae attach to rocks or the ocean floor. Then, those pebble-sized pieces of coral grow over many years to be larger than a school bus!

How many tentacles do octopuses have?

Octopuses have eight tentacles. These tentacles have many special skills, such as lifting heavy objects with the hundreds of suction cups they have. But these sea creatures can make eight tentacles seven if need be. Octopuses can detach a tentacle if a predator grabs hold of it, so they can escape. The octopus will just grow it back later!

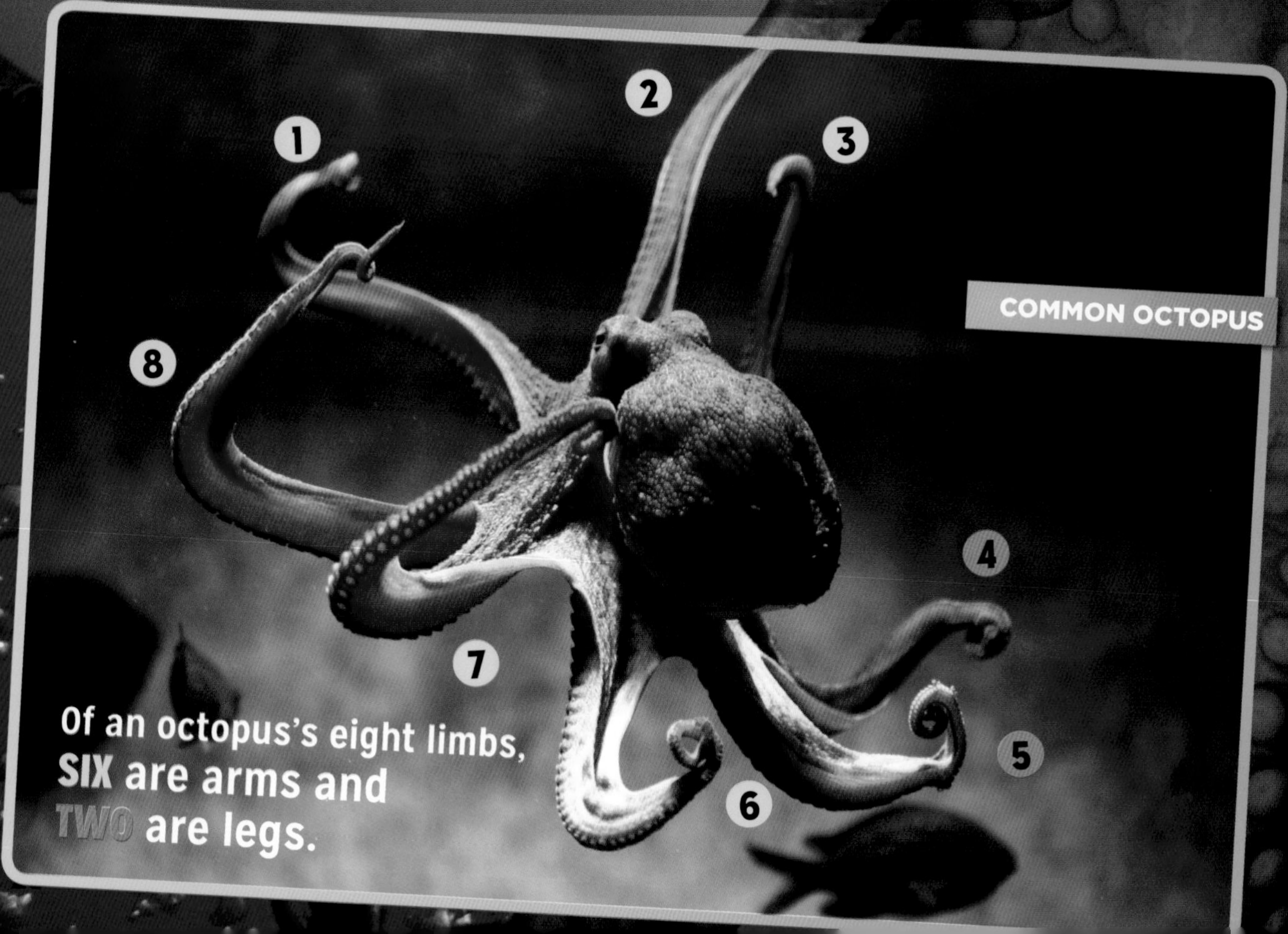

Of an octopus's eight limbs, SIX are arms and TWO are legs.

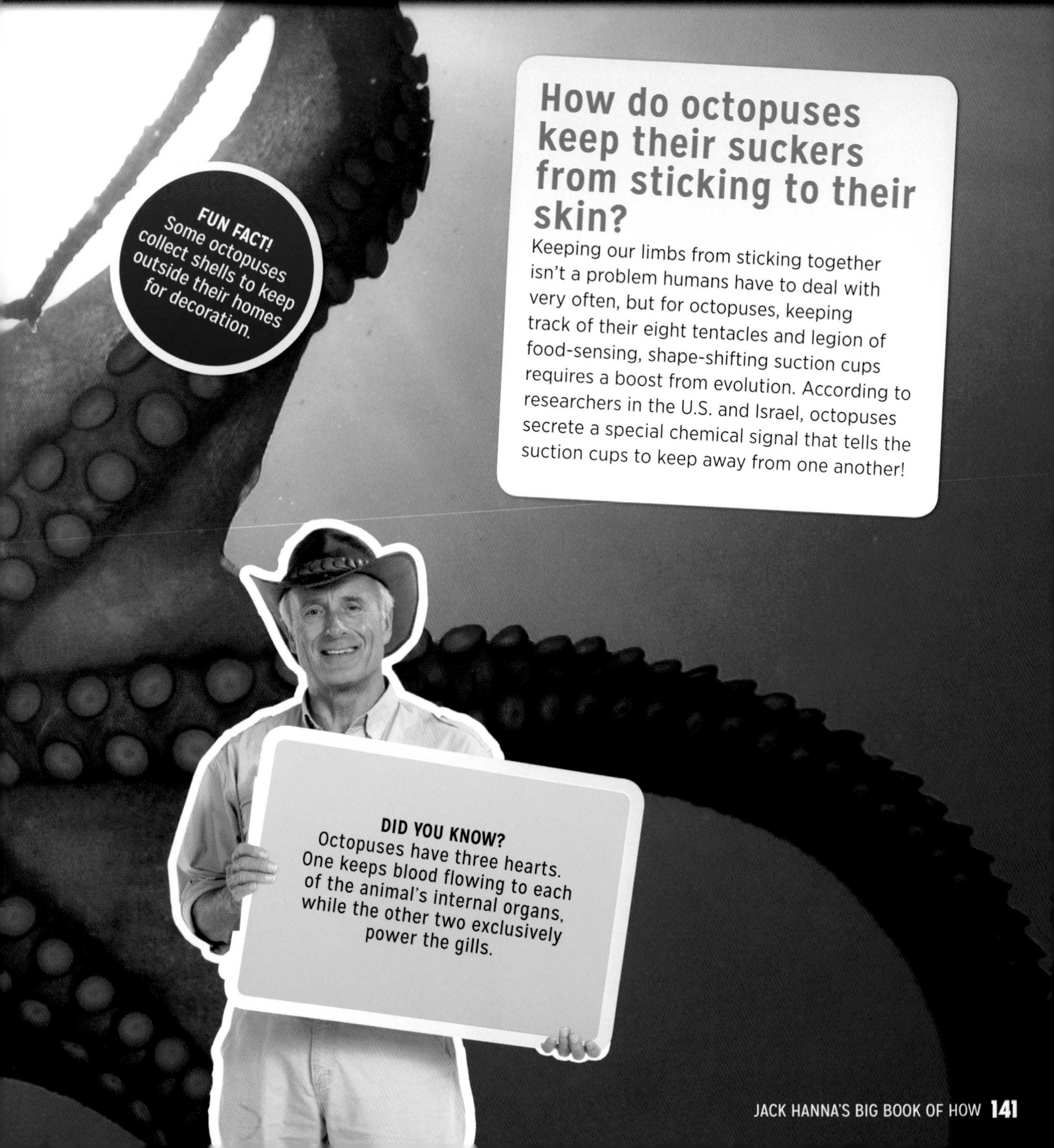

How do octopuses keep their suckers from sticking to their skin?

Keeping our limbs from sticking together isn't a problem humans have to deal with very often, but for octopuses, keeping track of their eight tentacles and legion of food-sensing, shape-shifting suction cups requires a boost from evolution. According to researchers in the U.S. and Israel, octopuses secrete a special chemical signal that tells the suction cups to keep away from one another!

FUN FACT!
Some octopuses collect shells to keep outside their homes for decoration.

DID YOU KNOW?
Octopuses have three hearts. One keeps blood flowing to each of the animal's internal organs, while the other two exclusively power the gills.

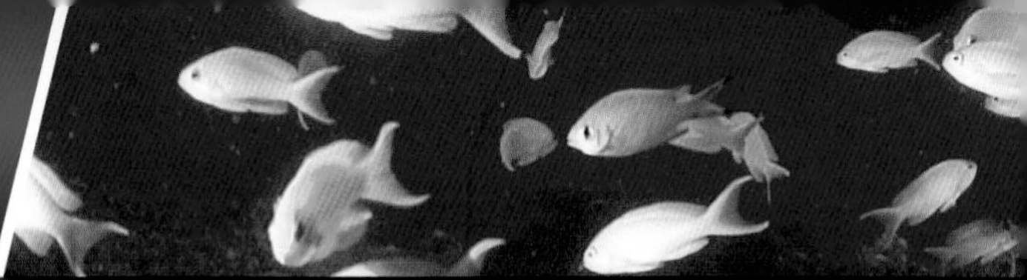

How do fish learn to swim?

Fish don't need to learn! Like we know how to breathe as soon as we're born, fish know how to swim. It's an instinct.

FUN FACT!
The ocean is filled with saltwater. Rivers and lakes are filled with freshwater.

ANTHIAS

How many fish live in the ocean?

You've probably heard someone say, "There are plenty of fish in the sea." Boy, is that true! There are more than 27,300 fish species in the ocean! Because so much of the ocean has yet to be explored, scientists don't know exactly how many fish live there.

How are freshwater fish and saltwater fish different?

Freshwater fish and saltwater fish have different levels of salt in their bodies. This means that their gills process water in a different way. They generally can't live in each other's habitats, but some fish, like salmon, can live in both fresh and saltwater!

How deep in the ocean do fish live?

It can vary! But most fish live no deeper than 600 feet in the ocean. The deeper you go, the weirder fish get. For example, get a load of the anglerfish!

YELLOW ANGLERFISH

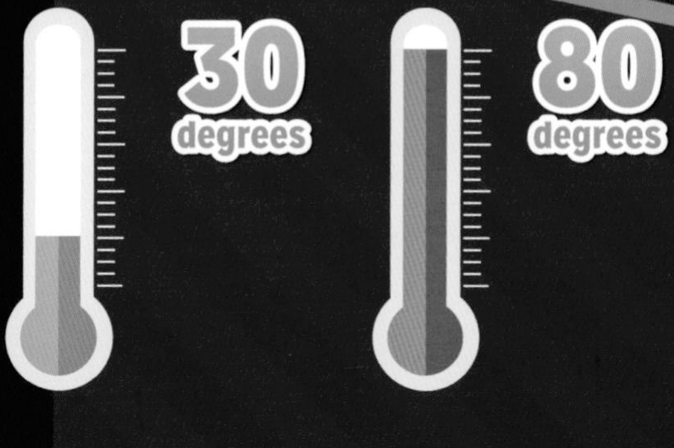

How cold is the ocean?

The ocean near Antarctica can be as cold as 30 degrees F, but near the equator, it can be as warm as 80 degrees F!

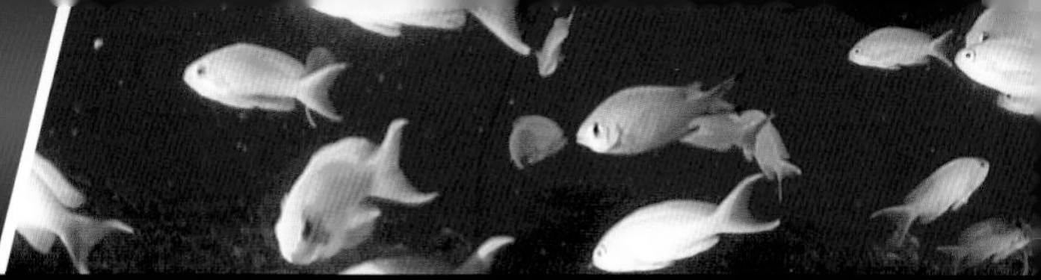

How do people take underwater pictures of animals?

My crew for *Jack Hanna's Into the Wild* uses special cameras that are made to film underwater! They allow us to get great footage of the animals that live in oceans all around the world.

PUZZLE

Underwater photographers must also be trained ______.

R I V E D S

Check your answers on page 172!

FUN FACT!
Filming for *Jack Hanna's Into the Wild* is always an adventure—we visited the island of Curacao to film their marine wildlife in 2013!

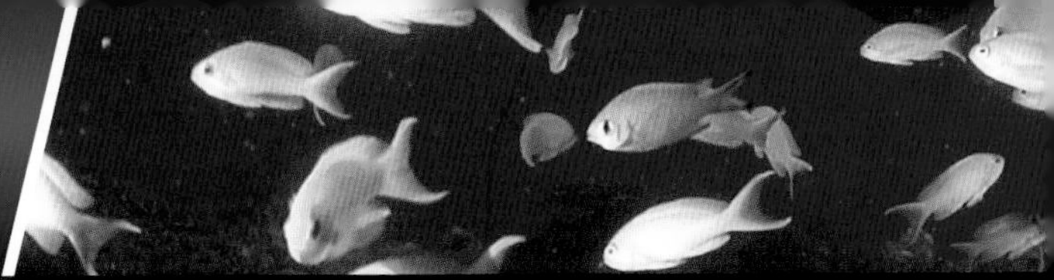

How do flying fish soar through the air?

Flying fish are shaped like torpedoes so they jet through the water with enough speed to break the surface. When they're in the air, they use their fins to help them "fly." They work like wings.

FLYING FISH

FUN FACT!
Flying fish can soar 4 feet out of the water and glide for distances of up to 655 feet—about the length of two football fields.

How do crab claws work?

Crabs use their claws like a human might use a Swiss army knife: one object that can do the work of many. Crabs can squeeze or crush things with their claws, use them as signals to communicate with other crabs, pick up food with them like chopsticks and even snip things like a pair of scissors.

How do seahorses use their twisty tails?

Seahorses have tails that are prehensile. That means that just like some monkeys, they can use them to grip things. For seahorses, this means using their tails to grip onto eelgrass, allowing them to stick their snouts into nooks and crannies in search of tasty treats.

How can you determine a fish's age?

In the same way you can count a tree's rings to tell how old it was, scientists can count the patterns on a fish's scales and calculate its age. As they grow older, fish scales gain new rings, called annuli, season by season. So by counting the rings, we can figure out how old the fish is!

How do fish chew their food?

Easy: They don't! Even fish lucky enough to have evolved teeth, including great white sharks, generally just use their teeth to hold prey in place while ripping off chunks to swallow whole. Smaller fish can simply open their mouths and let dinner float in, no chewing required.

Salutations from THE POLES

WHAT THIS HABITAT LACKS IN PLANTS IT MAKES UP FOR IN ANIMALS!

FUN FACT!
The ice in the Arctic holds about 10 percent of the world's freshwater supply.

The North Pole (in the Arctic) and the South Pole (in Antarctica) are at the top and bottom of the Earth, respectively. During some months in these regions, the sun never rises, and in other months it never sets!

It's cold down here—or up here. Where am I?

You'll find the Earth's poles at the very top and bottom of the world. The North Pole is in the Arctic, while the South Pole is in the Antarctic. The landscapes in both places are frozen and white. Summers up north can sometimes go above freezing temperatures, but otherwise, they usually stay below 32 degrees Fahrenheit. Believe it or not, tons of animals weather the cold!

FUN FACT!
Carrying an average of 30 pounds and standing as tall as 3 feet, the King is the second largest penguin, after the Emperor.

Penguins do all of their hunting in the water. What's the deepest a king penguin has ever dived for food?

- A 1,125 feet
- B 50 feet
- C 600 feet

Check your answers on page 172!

How often do penguins lose their feathers?

Penguins have special feathers that help them live in the Arctic. Their feathers basically act like wetsuits by trapping the penguin's body heat in and making them water and windproof! They might lose some here and there, but because these feathers do so much heavy lifting, once a year penguins have to spend two to three weeks on land shedding all of their feathers while new ones grow in! The process is called molting.

KING PENGUIN

DID YOU KNOW?
Penguins swallow a lot of saltwater, which they can't drink! Luckily, they have a special gland under their eyes that drips out the salt.

How much time do penguins spend in the water?

Penguins can spend several months at sea. The only reason they need land is to reproduce and shed old feathers. Air is another story, though! They have to come to the surface of the water to breathe.

GENTOO PENGUIN

How many different kinds of penguins are there?

There are 17 species of penguin! That's a lot of different types of black-and-white birds. Some of the best-known species are the emperor penguin and Galápagos penguin.

GALÁPAGOS

GENTOO

KING

How do penguins keep their eggs from freezing?

The South Pole is even colder than your freezer, which lingers around 5 degrees F. Down there, temps average around 56 degrees below zero on a typical winter day. That's no weather for a baby—even if it is a penguin! To protect their young, male emperor penguins balance their eggs on their feet and cover them with their feathered skin. Then, they stay that way for two whole months without eating or drinking!

How long does a narwhal's tusk grow?

This single tusk, which is actually a tooth, can grow to be up to 8.8 feet long. A narwhal's tusk is as long as an Asian elephant is tall! But only male narwhals' tusks grow this long. Sometimes a female will grow a tusk, but it won't be as lengthy. This tusk is one out of the two teeth narwhals have.

How do fish and whales stay warm in the ocean?

Fish, whales and other polar sea creatures have had 20 million years to adapt to the cold ocean temperatures. Many fish have a special chemical in their bodies that keeps their blood from freezing. Whales, belugas and seals are warm-blooded, so they can regulate their body temperature. They also have layers of fat, called blubber, that insulates them.

DID YOU KNOW?
Polar bears communicate with each other through a series of gestures. If you're watching a polar bear at a zoo, look out for their heads shaking side-to-side. This means they want to play! They also greet each other by touching noses.

How big is a polar bear?

A polar bear can grow as large as eight feet long and weigh up to 1,600 pounds! They're the largest member of the bear family. Even though they're massive and have a lumbering walk, over short distances they can run as fast as a galloping horse!

How many polar bears are left in the wild?

There are only about 26,000 left! The number of polar bears has been declining. That means they are ranked as a vulnerable species.

FUN FACT!
One polar bear usually weighs as much as two or three pianos!

How many cubs do polar bears have?

Polar bears usually have sets of twins when they give birth!

A polar bear cub is about the size of _____ when it's born.

- **A** A jelly bean
- **B** A stick of butter
- **C** A football

Check your answers on page 172!

How do animals get their names?

Actually, most animals have multiple names! Every animal has a scientific name, a common name and some nicknames! Take the *Bubo scandiacus*, for example! You probably know this little guy as a snowy owl or Arctic owl! Scientific names are written in Latin and Greek. They're a combination of the family an animal belongs to (*Bubo*) and the species it's given (*scandiacus*). Scientists choose the family based on characteristics. Common names and nicknames are less complex. They come from the way an animal looks or where it's found. Animals can even be named after the person who discovered them!

SNOWY OWL

PUZZLE

Snowy owls prefer to prey on this Arctic animal, whose name is scrambled below:

G E I N M L M

Check your answers on page 172!

How much do walruses weigh?

A fully grown walrus can weigh up to 3,000 pounds! That's about 10 big, bulky football linemen.

How do walruses get around?

Walruses use their strong flippers to paddle through the water and pull themselves across icy landscapes. When most people think of flippers, they think of the little flaps on the sides of walruses' bodies, but their tails are flippers, too!

How long are walrus tusks?

They can grow to be up to 3 feet long! Walruses need tusks so they can break through ice.

FUN FACT!
A walrus can have as many as 700 whiskers. And they never shave.

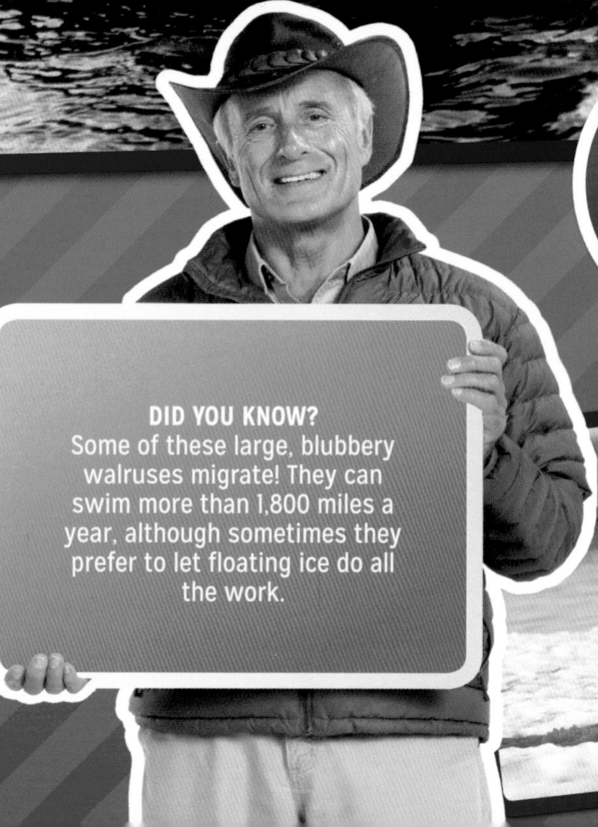

DID YOU KNOW?
Some of these large, blubbery walruses migrate! They can swim more than 1,800 miles a year, although sometimes they prefer to let floating ice do all the work.

ARCTIC FOX

FUN FACT!
Arctic foxes' fluffy tails are actually called brushes!

How do animals keep their white fur clean?

Polar animals live where almost everything is white, anyway, so it's not too tricky. When animals do need a bath, they groom themselves. They aren't very worried about how they look, though. Cleaning happens when animals are concerned about parasites or bugs making them feel sick or itchy. They usually lick themselves clean or go for a dip in water.

How are sea lions and seals different?

Sea lions have longer flippers, larger bodies and louder personalities than seals. Another difference is that sea lions have ear flaps, while seals don't have external ears at all. Finally, sea lions live in social groups, whereas seals prefer to live solitary lives in the ocean. How are they the same, you might ask? They're related because they both have fins for feet.

STELLER SEA LIONS

NEW ZEALAND FUR SEAL

ARCTIC FOX

FUN FACT!
A group of Arctic foxes is called a skull or a leash. Arctic foxes have roughly 6 to 12 pups at a time!

How warm does the North Pole get in the summer?

Temperatures can reach 32 degrees F in the summer, which is the temperature at which snow and ice begin to melt. When this shift happens, animals like the Arctic fox and snowshoe hare change their fur color from white to brown, so they can blend into their new environment better.

How do zoos keep animals warm when it snows?

Most animals at the Columbus Zoo and Aquarium have both indoor and outdoor living areas. For many warm-weather species, they need a place to go when it gets cold and snowy in Ohio, so they'll head to their indoor habitats where it's toasty all year round! Our polar bears, like the one to the right, spend a lot of time exploring their outdoor habitat and diving for fish in their pool, but even they retreat to their cozy indoor dens when they want to relax and stay warm!

How are reindeer different than normal deer?

Reindeer have tons of adaptations that white-tailed deer don't, which help them survive the harsh habitat they call home! Reindeer have thicker fur that helps them weather the cold and wide hooves that help them navigate the frozen landscape. Additionally, all reindeer have antlers, while only male deer do. Oh, and I almost forgot: Only one of these guys pulls Santa's sleigh!

Where do caribou live?

A Mexico

B Zimbabwe

C Canada

Check your answers on page 172!

FUN FACT!
Caribou migrate at least 600 miles each year to reach greener pastures!

How are reindeer and caribou different?

A lot of people confuse these cousins for one another. Most of the time, reindeer are domesticated, while caribou are wild. Another difference is that reindeer are smaller and more stout than their cousins.

BULL WOODLAND CARIBOU

How many Arctic wolves live in a pack?

Arctic wolves sometimes live in groups of up to 30! More often, though, seven to 10 wolves make a pack.

How are dogs related to wolves?

Both animals are members of the canine family. A long time ago, dogs and wolves shared an ancestor.

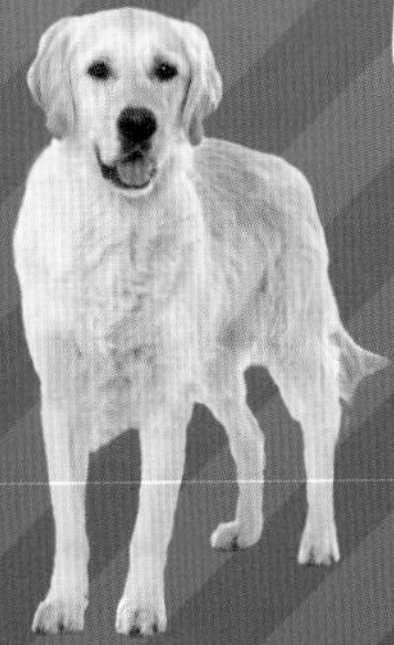

How are wolves and foxes different?

Wolves are bigger and more powerful than their fox cousins. Another difference is that foxes have partially retractable claws and bushy tails, but wolves don't.

How do search dogs find missing people?

The simple answer is their noses! Search dogs are trained to follow humans' scent to help find missing people.

FUN FACT!
A dog's sense of smell is impressive, but a salmon's sense of smell is thousands of times better. Yes—a fish!

How big are wolverines?

Wolverines are only about 16 inches tall and males can weigh around 50 pounds so they're roughly the size of a springer spaniel. But just because they're small doesn't mean they're not mighty! Wolverines have been known to bring down caribou and deer all by themselves. Their paws act like giant snowshoes, so while deer are sinking in the snow, wolverines are still running fast. They also have giant claws!

FUN FACT!
Even though their name sounds a little like wolf and it looks like a cross between a bear and skunk, wolverines are members of the weasel family.

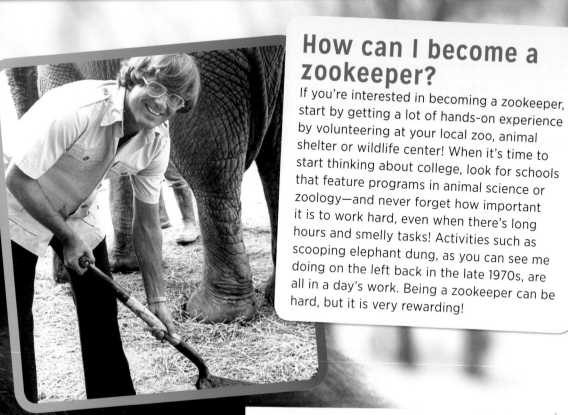

How can I become a zookeeper?

If you're interested in becoming a zookeeper, start by getting a lot of hands-on experience by volunteering at your local zoo, animal shelter or wildlife center! When it's time to start thinking about college, look for schools that feature programs in animal science or zoology—and never forget how important it is to work hard, even when there's long hours and smelly tasks! Activities such as scooping elephant dung, as you can see me doing on the left back in the late 1970s, are all in a day's work. Being a zookeeper can be hard, but it is very rewarding!

I have a lot of respect for the fierce wolverine, but during football season, you'll always find me rooting for the Buckeyes!

Media Lab Books
For inquiries, call 646-838-6637

Published by Topix Media Lab
14 Wall Street, Suite 4B
New York, NY 10005

Printed in China

ISBN-10: 1-942556-28-4
ISBN-13: 978-1-942556-28-2

All photos of Jack Hanna courtesy Jack Hanna. All other photos Shutterstock and iStock except: Suzi Hanna: p25, 105. Grahm Jones/Columbus Zoo and Aquarium: p33, 37, 41, 165, 171. Rick A. Prebeg/World Class Images: p58, 70, 145. Ron Foth Jr.: p81. Columbus Zoo and Aquarium: p171. Nature Picture Library/Alamy: p29. PCN Photography/Alamy: p32. Bradley Avison/The Noun Project: p43. Stefan Spieler/The Noun Project: p43. Sara Wright/The Noun Project: p82, 138. Karen Tyler/The Noun Project: p82, 138. Blickwinkel/Alamy: p83. Buddy Mays/Alamy: p100. Jane Wiley/The Noun Project: p137. Ates Evren Aydinel/The Noun Project: p137. Prisma Bildagentur AG/Alamy: p138. Wildlife GmbH/Alamy: p139. Robertharding/Alamy: p146. Age Fotostock/Alamy: p154. Nick Bluth/The Noun Project: p156. Alvarobueno/The Noun Project: p156. Boris Kiselev/The Noun Project: p156. Roger Eritja/Alamy: p166. Design Pics Inc/Alamy: p167.

Answer Key

How many quiz questions did you answer correctly? Use your new knowledge to test your friends!

Page 11: B
Page 15: C
Page 20: Fangs
Page 27: C
Page 34: B
Page 39: Meow
Page 42: C
Page 44: A
Page 46: Africa
Page 66: B
Page 71: A
Page 74: A
Page 83: B
Page 86: Mallard
Page 92: B
Page 96: India
Page 105: Gorilla
Page 110: C
Page 115: A
Page 116: A
Page 125: Blowholes
Page 130: C
Page 133: C
Page 136: Tongues
Page 144: Divers
Page 150: C
Page 157: B
Page 159: Lemming
Page 166: C

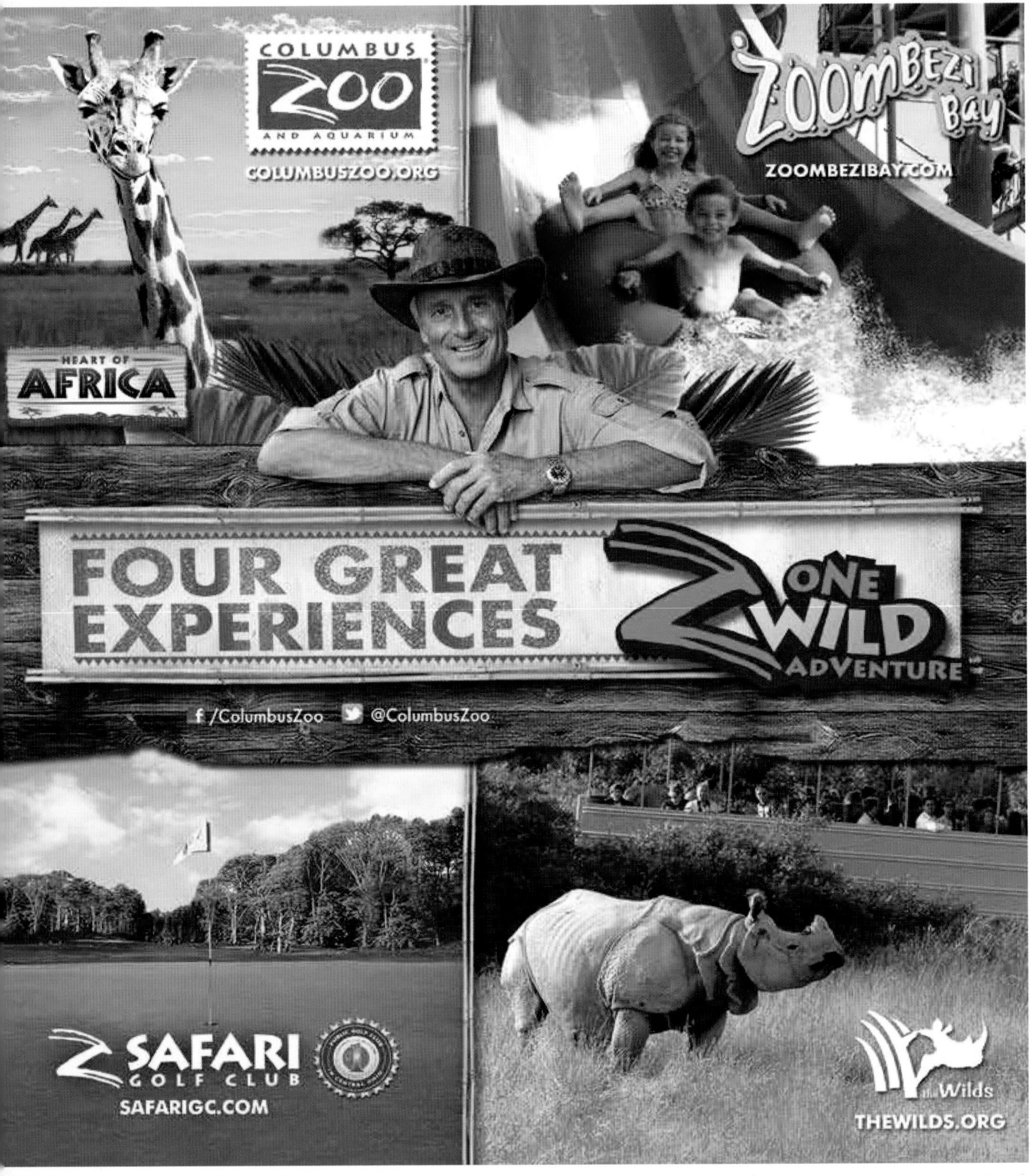

COLUMBUS
ZOO
AND AQUARIUM
COLUMBUSZOO.ORG
ZOOMBEZI Bay
ZOOMBEZIBAY.COM
HEART OF
AFRICA
FOUR GREAT
EXPERIENCES
ONE
WILD
ADVENTURE
f /ColumbusZoo
@ColumbusZoo
SAFARI
GOLF CLUB
SAFARIGC.COM
the Wilds
THEWILDS.ORG

ADOPT
Adopt an animal for yourself or a loved one at:
give.columbuszoo.org/adopt
adopt@columbuszoo.org
614.724.3497
$518
The monthly cost to feed a polar bear cub. As an adult, that will climb to $650!
30%
Reduction in polar bear population in the next 45 years if current patterns continue.
5
Animal Care Specialists who provided cub Nora round-the-clock care the first few months of her life.
1
Animal lover who can make a difference today: YOU!

TAKE A TRIP AROUND THE GLOBE WITH JACK HANNA!
Join nearly 3 MILLION HOUSEHOLDS watching Jungle Jack Hanna's exciting wildlife adventures from the comfort of your living room each weekend!
JACK HANNA'S WILD COUNTDOWN
Visit WildCountdown.com or tune into ABC stations this Saturday morning to catch the adventure!
JACK HANNA'S INTO THE WILD
Visit jhitw.com or check your local listings for show times.
presented by
Nationwide®
COLUMBUS ZOO AND AQUARIUM
Now available on-demand!
Search "Jack Hanna" on hulu, NETFLIX and amazon.com Prime

See you later,
alligator!